Talking to God Using Ten Psalms

Other Destiny Image Books by Elmer Towns

TALKING TO GOD
USING TEN PSALMS

Elmer Towns

DESTINY IMAGE® PUBLISHERS, INC.
PO Box 310, Shippensburg, PA 17257-0310
"Publishing cutting-edge prophetic resources to supernaturally empower the body of Christ"

This book and all other Destiny Image and Destiny Image Fiction books are available at Christian bookstores and distributors worldwide.

For more information on foreign distributors, call 717-532-3040.
Reach us on the Internet: www.destinyimage.com.

ISBN 13 TP: 978-0-7684-7729-0
ISBN 13 eBook: 978-0-7684-7730-6

For Worldwide Distribution.
1 2 3 4 5 6 7 8 / 28 27 26 25 24

CONTENTS

PREFACE
PREPARING YOUR HEART TO PRAY THE PSALMS

Psalms has 150 chapters, more chapters than any other book in the Bible. Most of the books in the Bible contain different topics like biography (study of people), history, sermons, and lectures; however, the Book of Psalms is made up of songs that can be sung. The psalms are sacred/solemn songs or hymns expressed in metric or musical rhythm. Basically, each psalm is a poem with devotional or spiritual meaning for your life. Most of the psalms are found in this one book of the Bible titled *The Psalms*, but you will find a sprinkling of other psalms throughout the Bible.

Many times, the psalms were sung or repeated dramatically to the tune of a psaltery. This is an ancient musical instrument with strings stretched on a flat surface or small box that was plucked with the fingers or struck with a bow that gives rhythm, movement, and melody.

Technically the word *psalm* in Hebrew is *tehillum,* which means "to make jubilant music." It comes from the root *halal,* which means "to yell greetings." Of course, this suggests a happy greeting. It is the word from which we get our present word *hello.* So how do you begin praying the psalms? You pray, "Hello, God." Of course, some psalms include solemn or mournful confessions of sin.

Also, some psalms were prayers; they represent all types of praying or praise to God, expressing happiness and joy. As mentioned above, some psalms are solemn prayers, expressing a somber mood or grief. The most important thing is that the psalms are attached to emotions and express our inner mood or the feelings when we are praying, singing, or chanting in words.

Therefore, the psalms have many purposes. Among their purposes you will find Psalm 23 is devotional; Psalm 119 is instructional; and then Psalms 3, 4, and 7 are complaints about an enemy.

PSALM

Each psalm is an event that brings you into the presence of God. And why do you come into God's presence? For many different reasons. Sometimes you come to ask, other times to thank Him for what He has done. Then at other times you come to give Him praise for answers to your prayer. Sometimes you are lonely and want His presence with you. Don't forget the time you were saved and you needed His deliverance or protection. Also, when you were lost and needed direction or confused and needed an answer.

Technically, a psalm is a worship event that expresses your heart or feelings as you come into the presence of God. So sometimes you use a psalm to express the feelings of your heart—maybe feelings you have difficulty putting into words.

The psalms in the Bible are like English poetry—its words have rhythm and meter. Years ago, I created a poem to tell my wife Ruth how much I loved her:

> As sure as the ivy grows round the stump,
> Ruth is my sugar lump.
> Roses are red, violets are blue,
> The angels in Heaven know I surely love you.

Now I recognize this juvenile expression reflected my heart and mind when I was young. The way we express our emotions changes as we grow. Feelings and emotions reflect our heart at the "now" when they are expressed or spoken.

HOW TO PRAY THE PSALMS

This book immerses you into a new experience with the book of Psalms. Usually, you read a particular psalm to understand its meaning, then you interpret what you read to understand what God is saying to you through the psalm. Then you try to apply its meaning/message to your life. But this book is different. When you are praying psalms, immediately interpret each verse to discover its meaning. Then you search the heart/mind of

God, who originally inspired the message of each psalm, to apply its meaning to your life. As you sing and repeat the words and music of each psalm, you find a new experience and you will discover God's presence speaking to you, singing to you. You find yourself listening to God. The end result of praying a psalm is enjoying intimacy with God.

When you read Psalm 90, you experience God's presence in life's struggles: "I the Lord have been your dwelling place throughout all generations, through physical difficulties and pain I will establish you" (see Psalm 90).

Next you read how God sees you through your suffering because you could "not forget" His promises of a future life with Him (see Psalm 137).

Then you pray for forgiveness (see Psalm 51) so your sin-pain will be wiped out and God will forget the agony of what your rebellion meant to Him.

Finally, you begin to experience relief from the gnawing pain of your sin and you are relieved of its agony when you rejoice in God. Because "God has searched me and known me. Where can I flee from Your presence? But how precious are Your thoughts to me" (see Psalm 139).

Next, you rejoice in prayer as you enter God's presence in Heaven, entering His gates with thanksgiving for His everlasting mercy (see Psalm 100). What else can you do but shout your happiness and joy as you enter His presence?

Then you enter the tabernacle of His presence with a heart full of worship, knowing one day in God's presence is better than a thousand days anywhere else. You are extremely happy to be God's doorkeeper, enjoying His presence (see Psalm 84).

As you get close to the Lord, you find He is a loving Shepherd to His sheep—to you especially. He protects you, feeds you, makes you lie next to Him to enjoy His presence (see Psalm 23).

When you look into your heart you will see many different types of feelings. The average person can quickly go from anger to sorrow, from rejoicing to bitterness, from laughing to weeping. It depends on the circumstances, our inner feelings at the time, and the situation at hand.

Therefore, when you begin to read the Psalms, do not read them like any other book or chapter in the Bible. Psalms responds to the entire range of human emotions, so read and interpret each psalm within its content when written. Then apply it to your situation at the time you read. Express your feelings through the words of each psalm.

INTRODUCTION
GETTING READY TO PRAY THE PSALMS

The psalms are a rich and deep tapestry (like the weaving of a most beautiful cloth) of the vast expressions of human need for God. The psalms express our praise, worship, and adoration, but they also express our deep guilt, anxiety, and deepest fears. The psalms express the happy times of life as well as the sad times, when we feel life has crushed us and we cannot go on.

God has given us the Book of Psalms to praise Him, to mediate on Him, and also to instruct us of His goodness and mercy. Psalms expresses our anger as well as our happiest moments of life. As one writer said, "Psalms expresses all of life and speaks to all of life."

Psalms teaches us how to pray and talk with God. Psalms expresses our adoration and praise for the majesty and holiness of God, yet at the same time Psalms expresses our yearning to know God intimately, walk with Him, and have His will done in our life.

Do you want to live a holy life in a sinful world? Then read and pray the psalms, and you end up praying as Jesus prayed, "Deliver us from the evil one."

Speak the psalms, pray the psalms, but most of all let's learn to worship God with the psalms.

Remember, the words of the Bible are Spirit-inspired, so each word in the psalm is given to us by God to tell us about God and how we should approach God. Since every word in every psalm is given to us by God, think each word, apply each word, pray each word, and obey each word.

The psalms will greatly enrich our spiritual depth and breadth, and we will learn from the example of the psalmist how to wait for God, hope in God, pray to God, trust in God, but most of all how to serve God, obey God, and do His will.

Remember, some psalms were prayers—all types of prayers, for all types of people, at all types of times. But other psalms were just devotionals to focus our thoughts on God, so we become spiritual in serving Him. Other psalms were complaints about the enemy and the attacks the psalmist was having in his personal life.

THE ARE MANY WAYS TO PRAY THE PSALMS

1. *Worship.* Isn't worship a compliment to God? We come to tell God how great He is, how magnificent is His nature, and how good are His thoughts and words to us. *"Come let us worship and bow down; let us kneel before the Lord our Maker"* (Psalm 95:6 NLT). So when you come to worship God, what are you doing? You are giving God the *worth-ship* God deserves because of who He is.

2. *Forgiveness.* Because we are all sinners and we all fall short, we need forgiveness all the time, in every area of our life, completely, eternally. *"According to the multitude of Your tender mercies, blot out my transgressions"* (Psalm 51:1 NKJV). And how much does God forgive? *"Who forgives all your iniquities"* (Psalm 103:3 NKJV). But there is more than forgiveness with God; He not only forgives us but He also wants us to love Him and fear Him at the same time. *"But there is forgiveness with You, that You may be feared"* (Psalm 130:4 NKJV).

3. *Surrender.* This is when you completely yield yourself to God. You pray the words of the Lord's Prayer, *"Your will be done"* (Matthew 6:10 NKJV). And how do you surrender? You ask for God's leadership in your life; *"He leads me beside the still waters"* (Psalm 23:2 NKJV).

4. *Protection.* This is asking the Lord to watch over and care for you. *"This poor man cried out, and the Lord heard him, and saved him out of all his troubles"* (Psalm 34:6 NKJV). Did you see the word *trouble* is plural? We not only have different pressures in life, but we also have different kinds of trouble, and all of our troubles are different in the pressure they bring us.

5. *Guidance.* This is needed to get help with decisions and problems. Be-fore you pray for help, remember God promises to be with you, to

protect you, but most of all to guide you. *"I will guide you"* (Psalm 32:8 NKJV).

6. *Victory.* We not only can face our troubles, endure our troubles, and finally get through our troubles, God also promised us victory over our troubles. He has promised to help us overcome sin (see Psalm 51), as well as answer those who attack us or our enemies (see Psalm 7). *"Through God we will do valiantly, for it is He who shall tread down our enemies"* (Psalm 60:12 NKJV). And what do you have when you achieve victory? *"I will dwell in the house of the Lord forever"* (Psalm 23:6 NKJV). This is a picture of having fellowship with Him, dwelling in His presence, and enjoying His protection.

7. *Provision.* We pray many prayers—we pray for victory, for things, for money, and we also ask God to provide all the needs of our life. *"The Lord has been mindful of us; He will bless us"* (Psalm 115:12 NKJV).

8. *Blessing.* This is God adding value to your life and all you do. *"O Lord, when I cry...have mercy also upon me, and answer me"* (Psalm 27:7 NKJV). Always hang on, for God will answer, but sometimes we need to call before He responds; we need to pray before He will answer. *"I would have lost heart, unless I had believed that I would see the goodness of the Lord..."* (Psalm 27:13 NKJV).

SELAH: PAUSE AND MEDITATE

Selah is one of the words used when we pray to God. Sometimes it is used by the psalmist who is praying to God to accentuate what he wants from God by crying out *selah*. Other times, after the psalmist has prayed to God, he cries *selah,* which means "I surrender" or "I yield my answer to the Lord." In this sense, *selah* is a substitute for *amen.* So when you pray *selah,* you are praying the same when you say *amen*—you are saying, "So be it, Lord," or "Have Your way, Lord," or "I yield to You, Lord."

Selah comes from two roots words/phrases—"to praise" and "to lift up." Therefore, it means to lift up God in praise.

The psalmist cried *selah* many times in the middle of the psalms; therefore, some think it was a musical note. But it was more than music; the psalmist was expressing the truth he knew. He was thinking out the content of his prayer and asking God to make it happen in his life.

Therefore, *selah* is a *thought-link*. When the psalmist prays *selah*, he is looking back at what he just said, and it becomes the basis for his praise. But also, the psalmist is looking forward to the next thought he is going to pray and the next request he is going to make to God.

But there is another meaning for the word *selah*. Sometimes it just meant to pause when you are praying. Stop praying and think about God to whom you are praying.

Then again, *selah* also means to lift up, which means as you pray you get louder as in a crescendo. That means you are building up to a great climax of worshiping God.

Jerome, one of the early church fathers, translated the word *selah* as "forever." When he cried out *selah,* he said, "God is eternal and forever." However, many contemporary church fathers translate the word *selah* to mean *amen.*

KINDS OF PSALMS

There are many different kinds of psalms, each one with a different meaning, each one with a different purpose. However, each psalm is a worship event because it focuses the psalmist away from himself to God. Whereas the psalmist might begin focusing in on his own needs and his sins, he ends up in the presence of God and ends up praising and magnifying God who is the Forgiver of all sin.

Synonymous poetry. When you are praying, you repeat yourself, such as the first verse is repeated in the second verse. *"Hear this, all peoples; give ear, all inhabitants of the world"* (Psalm 49:1 NKJV).

Antithetic poetry. The word *antithetic* means "the opposite." Therefore, the thought of the first phrase of the poem is the opposite of the second line. *"The wicked borrows and does not repay, but the righteous shows mercy and gives"* (Psalm 37:21 NKJV).

Synthetic poetry. This poetry deals with making a statement, then the first phrase becomes the basis for the second line, and it completes the thought of the author. *"The law of the Lord is perfect, converting the soul; the testimony of the Lord is sure, making wise the simple"* (Psalm 19:7 NKJV).

Climactic poetry. The idea of the first line is repeated and builds in the second line to a conclusion in the second or third line. *"Blessed is the man who walks not in the counsel of the ungodly, nor stands in the path of sinners, nor sits in the seat of the scornful"* (Psalm 1:1 NKJV).

HOW TO PRAY THE PSALMS

Begin with your deep feelings. The Psalms were written from the heart of the psalmist to appeal to the heart of the reader; therefore, it is communication from heart to heart. Therefore, when you pray the Psalms, it is from your heart to the heart of God, from heart to heart. Open up your heart to God, not just your head or your logic, not even your prepared prayer. Is your open heart to God's heart?

Each day as you read the Psalms, talk to God with the words you read and let those words touch your heart so that you can touch God. Remember, there are all types of depths to emotions. Some emotions are very shallow; they are right on the surface, and we cry easily; just as easily we laugh. Other emotions are deep and reach to the very heart and core of our life. Sometimes we have buried some things so very deep within ourselves we do not know about them, but the psalm may touch that hidden grief, and God brings mercy and peace to you.

You need to focus on God and talk to Him. The primary purpose of the Psalms is not to always understand the words or to try to interpret the meaning of the words as we might do when reading Paul's instructional epistles. No, when praying the Psalms, you focus on God and you talk to Him. You bring your emotions, express your emotions, and before it is all over, you pour out all of your emotions into the presence of God. To do this, let the psalm express your feelings to God.

CHAPTER 1
PSALM 23: IN GOD'S PRESENCE

Because You are my Shepherd
I commit my needs to You.
Provide green pasture for me to rest in,
And still waters to quench my thirst.
Restore my soul when I am empty,
And lead me in right paths for Your name's sake.
Be with me in danger when I walk
Through the valley of the shadow of death.
Deliver me from evil,
And protect me with Your rod and staff.
Prepare a table to feed me.
So my enemies can see Your provision.
Anoint me with the oil of Your healing,
Let me drink from the full cup of Your provision.
Surely goodness and mercy will always follow me,
And I will live with You forever.

—Psalm 23 ELT

WHEN THE LORD IS YOUR SHEPHERD

A Sunday school teacher visited a young boy from his class who was dying, "What hope can I give him?" the frustrated teacher thought. He didn't know what to say to the boy, because he didn't know how to prepare a young soul to die. Toward the end of his visit, the teacher reminded the young boy, "Remember, the Lord is your Shepherd."

Then to make it practical so the boy would remember the lesson, the teacher asked the little boy to hold up five fingers. Pointing to each of the five fingers, the teacher repeated the five words that begin Psalm 23, "The Lord is my Shepherd." Then the teacher asked the boy to repeat the phrase, touching each finger as he said the corresponding word. When the little boy counted to the ring finger—the fourth finger—he grabbed his chubby finger with his other hand repeating, "My. My Shepherd. The Lord is *my* Shepherd."

The next morning the little boy didn't wake up; he was asleep in Jesus. The parents found his chubby hand still holding the fourth ring finger. Truly in death, the Lord was *his* Shepherd.

> *The Lord is my Shepherd;*
> *I shall not want* (Psalm 23:1 NKJV).

When you say, "my Shepherd," you are admitting that you are a sheep, or at least you act like a sheep and have the needs of a sheep. If you have the characteristics of a sheep, your biggest need is a shepherd, because sheep can't make it in life without someone to lead them, protect them, and care for them. *Lord, I need You.*

What kind of shepherd would you choose if the choice were up to you? Obviously, sheep don't choose their shepherd, but let's just take a couple of minutes to play *what if.* Now you are a sheep, *what if* you could choose a shepherd? Tell me, what kind of shepherd would you pick? Before you do that, let me tell you what you shouldn't choose.

Your shepherd shouldn't be like a businessman; he'd want to make a profit off you. Your shepherd shouldn't be like an army sergeant; he'd want to lead you into battle. Your shepherd shouldn't be like a coach; he'd want you to win the game. Also, you wouldn't even want a king; he'd rule you.

None of these! You'd want a personal shepherd who loved you, not one who made money off you. And you'd want a shepherd who would protect you, not one who'd get you killed in battle. You would choose a shepherd who knew what you liked to eat, where you liked to go, and who knew how to care for you when you were sick. He'd know how to protect you from parasites, predators, and poison weeds. You'd choose a shepherd who would find comfortable places for you to sleep. If you got lost, you'd choose a shepherd who was brave and unselfish; he'd come looking for you. *Lord, I'm glad You first chose me.*

Isn't it good to know that you don't have a choice, but the Shepherd chooses you? When you say, "my Shepherd," you're not just telling everyone that the Lord is your personal Shepherd, but you're saying more than that. You're telling everyone you belong to the Shepherd who owns everything. He's "the Lord," and what does the Lord own? Everything! Your Shepherd is really big in this world, He owns it all. Your Shepherd owns everything because He created it all—everything. So you shouldn't worry about anything. *Lord, I want to be Your sheep.*

Are you in a hot, sweltering desert? He created the burning deserts as well as the cool, shaded pastures with crystal clear water. He knows where everything is located, and He can lead you to relief without looking at a map. *Lord, I need some water.*

Are you lost in a black valley and you see a *death shadow* behind a rock? You may not know where you are, but He knows. You're not lost to Him; He knows where you are in the valley because He created the valley. You can't even get lost in the dark night because the Lord even says, "I created darkness" (see Isaiah 45:7). You may have lost your way, but not the Lord. So take heart; help's coming. *Come quickly, Lord.*

Even after falling into a hole, you think no one in this world knows the trouble you're in. You're miserable in the hole because you think no one can help you—not your mother, not your buddy, not your spouse, not even a pastor. You're discouraged because the Lord is sitting on a throne up there in Heaven and you're mired in a hole. Wrong! Your Shepherd is the Omnipresent Lord. He may be overseeing Heaven, but He's also beside you in the hole. "Thou art with me." You've got a Shepherd who is everywhere present at the same time, and best of all, "the Lord is your Shepherd." *Hello, Lord, I didn't see You standing there.*

When the Shepherd brings you home, He doesn't leave you outside the door; He doesn't spank you, nor does He send you to bed without your supper. Your Shepherd treats you better than you deserve, better than you expected. Because the Lord is good, your Shepherd is good to you. He loves you when you're good; He loves you when you stray from Him. Because God is love, He will always love you. *And Lord, I love You.*

You've got a wonderful Shepherd; do you know His name? Because a person's name usually tells something about them, you ought to know your Shepherd's name. Why? So you can know Him better.

Your Shepherd's name is *Immanuel*, which means "God with us." He is not just the Lord high and exalted in Heaven. The Bible promises, "Unto us a child is given. Call his name Immanuel" (see Isaiah 9:6). Your Shepherd was conceived in a young virgin girl and born in the lowly stable where animals were kept, including sheep like you. His crib was a feeding trough for animals and sheep like you. He was confined to live in a human body, and He never once sinned. He got hungry, thirsty, and became so tired He fell asleep in the bow of a boat. Some ask how would God act if He became a man? Look at *Immanuel*, He is "*God with us.*" *Lord, thank You for coming to show me how You would live in the flesh.*

Your Shepherd's name is *Redeemer*. When you landed in the pawnshop of sin, your Shepherd walked in with the pawn ticket to pay the redemptive price to release you. The Bible says, "You were redeemed with the precious blood of Christ" (see 1 Peter 1:18-19). *Lord, I'm glad Your blood paid the price of my sin.*

Your Shepherd's name is *Deliverer*. Because you disobeyed God's laws, you were heading for punishment. You were heading for hell. What did your Shepherd do? He went after you and the Bible says He *"delivered us from so great a death"* (2 Corinthians 1:10 NKJV). *Lord, I'm glad You delivered me from hell.*

Your Shepherd's name is *Savior*. Because the Bible says, "All have sinned," this included you. Because the Bible says, "The wages of sin is death," you were lost with no hope, but your Savior reached His hand way down to save you from sin. *"The Father has sent the Son as Savior of the world"* (1 John 4:14 NKJV). *Lord, I'm glad You're still saving people, including me.*

How do you describe your Shepherd? Is he tall, skinny, old, or athletic? If you've got a Shepherd, you ought to know what he looks like.

The appearance of your Shepherd is not described in the Bible, even though He was once a baby in Bethlehem, and He died in the full strength of mankind on a cruel cross. He was not described because His appearance is not important, even though "He's the fairest of ten thousand" and

"He's altogether lovely." You'll learn His description by learning some of the things He does for you.

Your Shepherd is described as *"the door"* and *"the way"* because *"narrow is the door and straight is the way that leadeth to life, and few find it"* (Matthew 7:14 ELT). He will lead you to Heaven. *Lord, show me the way.*

Your Shepherd is described as *"the light of life."* Remember, it's a dark, scary world when you don't know where you're going, and there are dangerous pits along the way. When you get lost in the valley, your Shepherd has light. *Lord, shine some light over here on my feet.*

Your Shepherd is described as *"the resurrection"* because one day you'll die. *"It is appointed for men to die once"* (Hebrews 9:27 NKJV). No one wants to die, but your Shepherd died so you might live. And when you die, He'll raise you up in the last day. *Lord, I'm counting on You.*

Your Shepherd is described as *"the bread of life."* When you get hungry along life's path, don't complain. Go looking for your Shepherd because He said, *"He who comes to Me shall never hunger"* (John 6:35 NKJV). Isn't it good to know that you'll never get *soul-hungry* because He will satisfy you? You may miss a meal or two—and some martyrs starved to death physically—but your Shepherd will give you real *soul-satisfaction. Lord, I want to be satisfied with You.*

Your Shepherd is described as *"living water."* Do you ever get thirsty—not thirsty in your throat, but thirsty in your soul? When you do, it's *soul-thirst.* It's when you've taken a drink of cool water, but your heart is still empty, your soul is still scared, you still don't know what to do. Your Shepherd said, *"Whoever drinks of the water that I shall give him will never thirst"* (John 4:14 NKJV). Is your throat a little dry? Do you need some *"shepherd water"* to soothe your parched tongue? *Lord, I gladly drink from Your cup.*

Your Shepherd has a name. It wasn't given to Him like your parents probably gave you a name. Your Shepherd's name came from Heaven. An angel visited a young virgin maiden to tell her, *"The Holy Spirit will come upon you and you will conceive a son"* (Luke 1:35 ELT). Then the angel told Mary, "[You] *shall call His name Jesus"* (Luke 1:31 NKJV). Your Shepherd's name is Jesus.

You have a kind Shepherd. When vicious, self-proclaimed executioners wanted to stone to death the woman captured in the act of adultery, Jesus wouldn't let them do it. He told the woman, "Go and sin no more." Isn't that the kindness you need?

Your Shepherd can take care of sickness. When a woman sneaked up behind Jesus to touch the hem of His garment, she was immediately healed. Do you need a Shepherd who will look after your wounds?

Your Shepherd can get you out of trouble. Remember when the disciples thought they'd die at sea in a storm? Jesus came walking to them on the water because they were afraid. Then He calmed the storm to save them. Wouldn't it be comforting to have someone that strong to get you out of trouble?

When the multitude ran out of food, what happened? Jesus fed them with five loaves and two small fish. Wouldn't it be wonderful to have a Shepherd who would make sure you never went hungry?

What kind of Shepherd do you want? You want one who knows you. "*He* [Jesus] *calls his own sheep by name*" (John 10:3 NKJV). You want a Shepherd who knows the future: "*He* [Jesus] *brings out his own sheep, he goes before them*" (John 10:4 NKJV). You want a Shepherd who lets you pursue life, liberty, and soul-happiness.

Your Shepherd is the Almighty Lord God, your protection and guide. But your Shepherd made the most incredible sacrifice in history. He was sinless, but He gave His life for sinful people like you. He didn't like the idea of dying any more than you do, because He prayed, "*Father, let this cup pass from Me; nevertheless, Your will be done.*" Then He allowed soldiers to slap Him, beat Him with a leather whip, crown Him with needle-sharp thorns, then finally the soldiers nailed His hands and feet to a cross. His strength was drained as He hung six hours in the blistering Palestinian sun. A mob ridiculed Him. Even then they didn't kill Him. "*He said, 'It is finished!' And bowing His head, He gave up His spirit*" (John 19:30 NKJV). Your Shepherd voluntarily gave up His life for you. He said, "*I lay down My life that I may take it again. No one takes it from Me*" (John 10:17-18 NKJV). *I need an unselfish Shepherd like Jesus.*

But your Shepherd wasn't conquered by death; they carried His dead body into the grave, but He walked out alive three days later. Now He can give you victory over death and despair. When you face death's dark valley,

He will walk with you through death's door and out the other side because He's already been there. Don't you love Him? *Lord, I do!*

Your Turn to Pray

> *Lord, I live in my little world, looking after my family,*
> *my business, my reputation, and my friends;*
> *thank You for helping me do these things.*
> *Lord, You are all-powerful, all-knowing, and everywhere present,*
> *yet You condescended to be concerned about my little world and You*
> *care about my insignificant troubles;*
> *I praise You for Your love and kindness.*
> *Lord, You are the great God of the universe;*
> *Your holy name is pure and Your majesty is awesome, yet You are kind*
> *and gentle to me. I don't understand why, but I humbly accept Your*
> *love.*

Some people say, "The Lord is *'a'* shepherd," suggesting that they only know Him as one shepherd among many. But you cannot have many shepherds; there can only be one Shepherd and only one path to Heaven. Jesus said, *"I am the way.... No one comes to the Father except through Me"* (John 14:6 NKJV). There are not many roads to Heaven, and there are not many ways to God, and there are not many shepherds. The Lord is the *only* Shepherd. Can you say, "The Lord is my Shepherd"?

You shouldn't even say, "The Lord is *'the'* Shepherd," suggesting by the article "the" that the Lord is the unique Shepherd. While there is some truth that "the Lord is *the* Shepherd," it misses what is taught in Psalm 23—*intimacy*. The Lord really wants you to do more than identify Him as the great God; He wants a personal relationship with you. He wants you to say, "the Lord is *my* Shepherd." Why does He want you to say that? Because that's who He is. *Lord, I thank You for being my Shepherd long before I recognized it.*

And don't say, "the Lord is *'our'* Shepherd," even though that is a true statement. In church we pray, "Our Father who art in Heaven," using the plural pronoun "our" to show that we are one among many who come to Him in prayer. But when you pray Psalm 23, you are not one in a crowd; you're not even one in a church congregation. You are the only one who matters, because you belong to the Shepherd and the Shepherd belongs personally to you. When you relate personally to the Lord, nothing else matters. *Lord, You are mine.*

Why must you have a personal shepherd, and why must the Shepherd give you personal attention? Because serpents slithering through the grass will poison sheep, and wolves watching in nearby caves will attack sheep, and rushing water will drown sheep, and there are high places where sheep can fall to their death. And besides all that, sheep walk through dark threatening valleys where *death shadows* stalk them. You need a Shepherd, so remember *the Lord is your Shepherd-Protector.* He is not just any type of shepherd; He is *your* personal Shepherd who cares for you and will protect you.

Some people think the Lord is their Shepherd if they don't sin, but that's not what Psalm 23 says. Other people think the Lord is their Shepherd if they read the Bible, pray, and give their money to church. No matter where the sheep stray, they belong to the Lord, and the Shepherd will go seeking His sheep. We've never read of the Shepherd kicking a single sheep out of His care, nor have we ever read that the Shepherd ever refused to go look for a stray sheep. Why? Because the sheep belong to Him. *Lord, You are my Protector and I belong to You.*

Picture a sheep in the meadow: it doesn't worry about where the food is for next week, tomorrow, or even in the next few minutes. Sheep rely on the shepherd for good green grass and pasture. Sheep don't worry about predators in the rocks because it's the shepherd's job to worry about protection. The sheep don't have to worry about the coiled snakes, deep water, or high places. *Thank You, Lord, for protecting me.*

Do you have problems? The question is not how you're going to solve them. If you have problems, the question is *relationship.* Do you know the Lord? Are you His sheep? Stop grazing with your head down in the grass. Lift your head and look around. Do you see your Shepherd? If so, don't worry. It's His job to protect sheep; He will care for you. If you are His sheep, the problems belong to the Lord because of the promise, "The Lord is *my Shepherd.*" *Thank You, Lord, for Your constant care.*

Some people seem to say, "The Lord used to be my Shepherd." There are a lot of people who used to go to church, who used to be a Sunday school teacher, or who used to be faithful. But something happened. When they had financial reversals, they turned their back on God, or they got sick and cursed God because of the pain. Whatever happened, they *used* to follow the Shepherd, but remember, the problem of the past-tense verb is with the sheep, not with the Shepherd. People stray away from the Shepherd, but the Shepherd does not leave the sheep. Remember, *the Lord is my nearby Shepherd.*

There's another verb to study—*will be*. Some people say, "The Lord will be my Shepherd in the future." Are you living in the future? Do you plan to get right with the Lord sometime in the future? Right now you're busy, you're having fun, you're starting a new job, you're studying for final exams. Your life is too hectic to say "the Lord is my Shepherd" because you'd have many changes to make. But you love the Lord and you know some day you'll need Him, so you say, "The Lord *will be* my Shepherd." Don't describe your relationship to the Lord by a future-tense verb. *Lord, I need You now.*

You can have a close relationship with the Lord today. His favorite time is *now*. You can touch the Lord *right here, right now, immediately! Thank You, God, for not being too busy for me.*

Your Turn to Pray

Lord, I have many problems. Some are like little stones in my shoe that are irritating; other problems are like huge boulders that I pretend are not there. I yield my problems to You—solve them for me.
Lord, You know what problems I will face tomorrow and next week; You know the coming storms that I don't even know about. Prepare me for them. I yield my future to You.
Lord, help me not live in the past tense, always remembering what You did for me in the past—do it again now.
Lord, I sometimes live in the future, always planning to do more for You when I get around to it;
I will live for You today.

If the Lord is not your Shepherd, then who is? Who shepherds you? If anyone or anything else is your shepherd, you will probably never find the satisfaction you seek in life. That doesn't mean you won't have fun at worldly gatherings, nor does it mean you won't experience the thrill of an accomplishment of a job or the pleasure when your child is born. But if the Lord is not your Shepherd, you will always want something else, something more, something bigger, better, faster, or more expensive.

If the Lord is not your Shepherd, when you get a promotion at work you will not be happy until you get another one—and another one. When you play the perfect game in sports, you will not be happy until you do it again. When you make your first million, you will not be happy until you get a second, and third, and fourth, etc. No matter what you do in this life, success begets a desire for more success, and you will never be satisfied. But when the Lord is your Shepherd, you will be able to honestly say in your soul, "I shall not want."

If your boss is your shepherd, then you will probably be restless or feverish with life's usual frustrations. As a matter of fact, your boss is placed over you to get the most out of you, and his job is to make you do your job. Your boss will never make you feel at rest or make you say, "I shall not want." As a matter of fact, when your boss feels you don't want any more—you don't want to improve, you don't want to contribute more, or you don't want to be a team player—he will fire you. So make the Lord your Shepherd, and you can honestly confess, "I shall not want."

Is education your shepherd? Then you will be constantly disillusioned. The pursuit of truth is a wonderful endeavor; you will become wise and confident. When you gain truth, like salt on your tongue it makes you thirsty for more. But until you know Jesus who called Himself truth, you will not really become happy with what you know or satisfied with who you are. But when the Lord is your Shepherd, you can testify, "I shall not want."

What about enjoyment of life—is fun your shepherd? If you make fun your shepherd, your life will be put on hold, like the unresponsive telephone—you never get through. The important thing to remember about fun is that fun is like the bubble you seek to hold in your hand; the moment you clutch it, it's gone. You go to the carnival to have fun, and there you laugh, scream, and you are thrilled with the animals under the big tent. For weeks you look forward to the carnival because it's coming to your town, and you anticipate an exciting time. When you're there, you have fun, but what happens after you leave the carnival? There is an emptiness in your heart. Must you repeatedly go back to the carnival to have fun? Surely you have memories of fun at the carnival, but do you want to spend your life looking at a scrapbook, remembering the fun times you used to have? It's no fun living in the past tense.

But when you know the Shepherd, He gives you enjoyment that's greater than fun; He gives you satisfaction and contentment. Jesus called it peace: *"Peace I leave with you, My peace I give unto You."* Now you can have an experience that's greater than fun; it's a trusting relationship with your Shepherd. When you rest securely at His feet, you don't need anything, you don't lack anything, you don't fear anything. It's peaceful at His feet. However, when fun is gone it's gone, and you have to seek it again to enjoy the experience again. But when you have His peace and contentment, it's continuous. You can say, "I shall not want today." As long as you have the Shepherd, you can say in all your tomorrows, "I shall not want, now." As long as you make the Lord your Shepherd, you will always have peace and contentment. *Lord, it's so peaceful lying at Your feet; I don't want to ever leave.*

Your Turn to Pray

> *Lord, I'm tired of looking for fun everywhere.*
> *I'm tired of dead-end streets and I'm tired of running on empty. Be my*
> *Shepherd so I shall not want any longer.*
> *Lord, I want to be happy, I want to be at peace with myself,*
> *I want to feel great; may I sit close to You?*
> *Lord, I want to please You and have fellowship with You;*
> *thank You for taking care of me and protecting me.*
> *Lord, it is so good to feel good and I feel good when I'm close to You.*
> *Help me stay here and keep me from straying.*

Chapter 2
Psalm 1: Two Ways to Live

Your life will be happier if you don't follow the advice of sinners, and you don't loiter with the wicked, and you don't become a part of an evil group. You will discover happiness by obeying My laws and thinking about Me day and night. You will be like a tree rooted by living waters, bearing fruit when you need it. Your leaf will not wither, and you will prosper in what you do. The wicked are blown about like worthless trash; I will judge them for their rebellion and wasted life. They will not stand with the godly before Me, for I take care of those who live right, but the evildoers will be destroyed.

—Psalm 1, author's paraphrase

The book of Psalms begins with the word *blessed*, which means happy. Therefore, this psalm, when read and memorized, can be used to help you live a happy life free of sin. Because David was a man after God's own heart, he enjoyed a happy life by putting God first in everything.

After all, what a person determines in life determines who he is and how he lives. Because David enjoyed worshiping God, he was a blessed man and a happy man.

Therefore, happy is the person who:

- Does not listen to bad advice of those rebelling against God;
- Does not spend his time doing evil with evil people;
- Does not join into the sin of sinners.

But David's happiness is doing what God tells him to do:

- He meditates on Scriptures day and night.

David as a young man learned to put God first in his life and to meditate/think about God all the time when he was watching the sheep out in the field. As a result, God chose him when he was very young to be the king of Israel. Now David is much older and he is writing to help other people achieve the happiness that he has achieved. He wants them to walk with God, know God, and obey God.

He knows when a person constantly worships God, they will be blessed—they will be a happy person.

> *Lord, I want to be like a tree planted by living waters. I want to bear fruit in the right seasons, so my leaves keep growing* (see Jeremiah 17:8).

There is always a negative side to following God. Those who follow God live a positive life, but those who reject God or refuse to do His will live a negative life of sin and transgressions.

There are always scoffers who make fun of those who follow God, and there are always the ungodly who disobey God, and finally there are always those who rebel against God in both words and action.

The ungodly are like dead husks that the wind blows away.

They shall be condemned in judgment and thrown out of the presence of God.

The Lord protects the life of the godly,

but the ungodly shall perish (see Psalm 23:4-6).

Life is divided between two types of people. There are those who want to follow the Lord, and those who will not follow the Lord but will walk their own way. Get a clear picture in your mind of two types of people: some people want to follow the Lord, but may have bad habits or occasionally sin, and their backsliding confuses those who observe them. On the other hand, there are evil people who may do good deeds, and at times they even go out of their way to help others.

The book of Psalms is poetry to express our feelings toward God and express our emotions. Psalms lets us look into the heart of God to understand Him, His explanations for our life, and our response to Him. Psalms begins with *"Blessed is the man who walks not in the counsel of the ungodly, nor stands in the path of sinners, nor sits in the seat of the scornful"* (Psalm 1:1 NKJV).

The book of Psalms begins by looking to God for His divine reaction to us.

When you bless another person, you are bestowing good or positive actions upon that person.

But at other times, "to bless" means you are requesting God to make something holy or for His presence/person to rest upon the personal thing being blessed.

When you are blessed, you are consecrated, divinely favored, and given God's happiness or God's goodness.

When God had Moses write the first word in the book of Psalms, a book that defined His heart, God chose to begin the first psalm and the whole book of Psalms with His passion for His people. God wants to give His heart to everyone who reads and obeys the book of Psalms.

Who is blessed of God? *"Blessed is the man who walks not in the counsel of the ungodly, nor stands in the path of sinners, nor sits in the seat of the scornful"* (Psalm 1:1 NKJV).

There are three types of people who will try to get you to deny God, disobey God, or at least displease Him, and these three people are mentioned in the first verse. First are the ungodly. These are people who are not like God, do not follow God, and are walking away from God. The Hebrew word *rasha* describes people who actively rebel against God. Do not stand near these people—their example will influence you to sin.

The second type of person is the one who stands in or near the path of sinners. The word is *chatta*, which is the Hebrew word that means those who have missed the mark. These are the ones who have not only left God, but they have also distanced themselves from God.

The third type of person is the one sitting in the seat of the scornful. This is *luwts*, the scorners. This evil group is using their mouths/words to mock God or verbally abuse those who follow Him. These people not only have walked away from God and disobeyed God, now they are the source of everything evil.

The psalmist is saying if you want to be close to God, be like a tree rooted by streams of living water.

Again, look at your Scripture to find the three sources of temptation. If a person is walking away from God, they have stopped following God. The second step is to loiter, which means that person is standing around temptation, not fleeing temptation. If you stand around temptation, usually you will give in to its attraction. The third group is sitting in the seat of the scornful. That person is no longer following God, and they are now surrounded by people who are also *scorning* God.

Now let's move away from the three groups of people and let's look at two comparisons. First is a tree planted by rivers of living water. What can be said about this tree? It has roots that seek water, take in water, and live. There is life in this tree and its roots are expanding.

Next, these growing trees had fruit, and what is fruit? Growing up in Savannah, Georgia, we had several trees in our yard that grew fruit. We had a pecan tree, plum tree, pomegranate tree, apple tree, and a crab apple tree. We did not plant those trees; they were there when we rented the house. Not only did I enjoy the fruit, but there were about seven to eight boys living in our neighborhood who always came over to help us enjoy these fruits from these trees.

KEY WORDS

1. Blessed (Psalm 1:1)

The word *blessed* is *asher*, which means "happy." The book of Psalms emphasizes the positive or productive life of those who are walking with God. Let's not confuse happiness and blessedness. Blessedness is joy that comes from God and that person is blessed when doing the right thing, for the right reason, at the right time. Blessedness is something you receive when you do what you want to do, but is found on the road to duty when you do what you are supposed to do. The Bible teaches there are seven things you can do to gain joy. First, delight yourself in the word of God and you will please Him (Joshua 1:8). You will be happy when you make the Bible the basis for principles by which you live.

2. You must obey the Bible.

This Book of the Law shall not depart from your mouth, but you shall meditate in it day and night, that you may observe to do according to all that is written in it... (Joshua 1:8 NKJV).

3. Make the Bible the basis for the principles by which you live.

But be doers of the word, and not hearers only, deceiving yourselves. For if anyone is a hearer of the word and not a doer, he is like a man observing his natural face in a mirror; for he observes himself, goes away, and immediately forgets what kind of man he was. But he who looks into the perfect law of liberty and continues in it, and is not a forgetful hearer but a doer of the work, this one will be blessed in what he does.

If anyone among you thinks he is religious, and does not bridle his tongue but deceives his own heart, this one's religion is useless. Pure and undefiled religion before God and the Father is this: to visit orphans and widows in their trouble, and to keep oneself unspotted from the world (James 1:22-27 NKJV).

4. Make the Bible the standard on which you base your salvation.

All Scripture is given by inspiration of God, and is profitable for doctrine, for reproof, for correction, for instruction in righteousness, that the man of God may be complete, thoroughly equipped for every good work (2 Timothy 3:16-17 NKJV).

5. Hear and obey the Bible.

Blessed is he who reads and those who hear the words of this prophecy, and keep those things which are written in it; for the time is near (Revelation 1:3 NKJV).

6. Feed on it to grow spiritually.

Peter, an apostle of Jesus Christ, to the pilgrims of the Dispersion in Pontus, Galatia, Cappadocia, Asia, and Bithynia, elect according to the foreknowledge of God the Father, in sanctification of the Spirit, for obedience and sprinkling of the blood of Jesus Christ: grace to you and peace be multiplied. Blessed be the God and Father of our Lord Jesus Christ, who according to His abundant mercy has begotten us again to a living hope through the resurrection of Jesus Christ from the dead (1 Peter 1:1-3).

7. Bring forth his fruit in his season.

How do you interpret the word "his"? Some interpret it to mean "God"— that He shall bring forth fruit in God's season. Other people think it is the person represented by the tree. So when he is planted by the rivers or living water, he will bring forth fruit in the appropriate season. Just as all fruit has a season when it is ripe and ready to be eaten, so the one who is planted by rivers of living water and abides with the Lord grows to full maturity.

CHAPTER 3
PSALM 51: A CRY FOR MERCY

*I will have mercy on you because of My unfailing love. I will have
compassion on you, and blot out the stain on your sin. I will wash you
clean from your guilt, and I will purify your soul. Because you recognize your rebellion against Me, your sin haunts you day and night.
Your sin was against Me, not others, but against Me; you have done
evil in My sight. You realize I am right in what I do and My decisions
about you are correct. You are a sinner, and were born in sin; you
have sinned since your mother conceived you. But I desire honesty even
in the womb, I began teaching you what to do even there. I will purify you and you shall be clean, I will wash you so you are whiter than
snow. Yes, I have broken you because of your sin, but I will give you
back your joy and rejoicing. I will not constantly remind you of your
sin, I will give you a clean heart and renew an obedient spirit in you.
I will not throw you out of My presence and I won't take the Holy
Spirit from you. I will restore the joy of your salvation, and give you
a willing spirit to obey Me. Then you can teach sinners My way, and
they will come to Me for forgiveness. I will forgive you for shedding
blood, then you can joyfully sing My praises. I will open your mouth
to speak for Me, and your lips will sing My praises.*

—Psalm 51:1-15, author's paraphrase

This psalm reveals David crying out for mercy from God because he had
sinned a terrible sin. He had planned the murder of Uriah. And why?
Because of his adultery with Bathsheba, Uriah's wife. David had sinned a
terrible sin by committing adultery with a married woman who was not
his wife. He had sexual relations with Bathsheba, who got pregnant. David
was trying to cover his sin by arranging for the death of Uriah in battle.
David's treachery was a sign of his hardness against repentance. As a result,

he had to live with sin in his life. If it came out that David was the father of Bathsheba's child, news of his sin would ruin his ministry as king of Israel. So David had Uriah killed in battle.

Yet the bold prophet Nathan came to stand before David. Nathan told David the story of a rich man who had many sheep, and a poor man who had only one lamb. When it came time for settling a legal debt, the poor man's only sheep was taken as payment. David responded in anger against the injustice. At that moment Nathan the prophet cried out, *"You are the man"* (2 Samuel 12:7).

When confronted with his sin, David became honest and broken before God; he knew he had sinned. It was then that David cried out, *"Have mercy upon me, O God, according to Your lovingkindness"* (Psalm 51:1 NKJV). When David asked for mercy, it was according to God's forgiveness and lovingkindness. The Hebrew word for forgiveness is *hesed*, which reflects God's deepest love. David made a "well phrased" request because he was asking for complete forgiveness. It was a result of his brokenness before God.

The Scriptures are clear: God has mercy—much more mercy than we have sins. If we have sins in great numbers, even as great as the hairs on our head, God's mercies are as great as the stars of the heavens—they cannot be measured, neither can God's mercy be limited. When David speaks of God's lovingkindness, he is describing God's unfailing love—love that cannot fail, has never failed, and will never fail in the future.

So when you come to describe God's tender mercies, look at His feelings. God has emotions, and He feels deeply, just as our sin causes us to feel deeply. But God feels as deep as His mercies and tender love, which are limitless. If God feels our infirmities, He does so infinitely. When David prayed "blot out my transgressions," he was using the saying *"blot me out of Your book which You have written"* (Exodus 32:32 NKJV).

Someone has observed that you are asking God to blot out the black lines of your sin with the red blood of His sufferings and death on the cross.

Then David asked, *"wash me thoroughly from my iniquity"* (Psalm 51:2 NKJV). Until a person can see how dirty and filthy his sins are in the sight of God, he is not ready to ask God to completely cleanse him from every stain and iniquity. When God used the word *thoroughly*, He is saying He wants the sin completely eradicated or eliminated so that He cannot see them, visit them again, or even think of them.

Then David cried, *"I acknowledge my transgressions"* (Psalm 51:3 NKJV). He was fully aware of his sinful condition before God. The emphasis here is on the word "I." Why was David convicted? *"My sin is always before me."* You can do your best to ignore your sin, deny your sin, or even try to pretend it never happened; but your sin remains in the presence of God. Until you see your sin through the eyes of God, you will not deal with it, confess it, or beg for forgiveness and cleansing.

David was a king, but his position and power and authority did not give him authority to remove the sin. Only God can deal with sin, and He does that by the blood of Jesus Christ.

David confessed, *"against You, You only, have I sinned"* (Psalm 51:4 NKJV). Yes, David had sinned with Bathsheba in committing adultery with her, and then he sinned against Uriah in taking his wife to bed. David's sin was against himself, and against his position as king and spiritual leader of the people of Israel.

So finally David came to himself when he said, *"against You, You only, have I sinned"* (Psalm 51:4 NKJV).

In David's eyes, he had tried to cover his sin because he was king, and he felt he was accountable to no one because he was king, but he was accountable to God. David originally saw his sin in his own eyes, but he was not looking through the eyes of God. Then David prayed, *"Purge me with hyssop, and I shall be clean; wash me, and I shall be whiter than snow"* (Psalm 51:7 NKJV). David was looking to God to do what only the Lord could do—make him spiritually and morally clean. Yes, David would go offer a sacrifice with a lamb for the substitute for his sins, but his heart drove him to seek full forgiveness in the presence of God. When David prayed to be *purged*, he is asking that the sin be completely wiped away so it would exist no more.

It is a terrible thing to be confronted with the blackness of your heart and the awfulness of your sin, but there is no comparison when you consider the joy and gladness that only God can give to a repentant sinner.

Notice how David repented and deeply asked for forgiveness and restoration: *"Hide Your face from my sins, and blot out all my iniquities"* (Psalm 51:9 NKJV).

Do not treat forgiveness as a light thing after you sin. God did not treat sin as a light thing when He allowed His Son to die on a cruel cross for your sins and mine.

So David asked repeatedly for forgiveness, cleansing, and restoration. This was not a light thing to ask, and David realized the eternality of sin's consequences as he begged from the bottom of his heart, repeatedly, for forgiveness and restoration.

> *Create in me a clean heart, O God, and renew a steadfast spirit within me. Do not cast me away from Your presence, and do not take Your Holy Spirit from me* (Psalm 51:10-11 NKJV).

Forgiveness was not enough for David; he also wanted complete restoration into God's presence. And he knew he had to have a clean heart to enter God's presence. So, more than cleaning, he needed renewal. David had lost his desire to seek God. Notice David's request, *"Restore to me the joy of Your salvation, and uphold me by Your generous Spirit"* (Psalm 51:12 NKJV). Remember, there was time after David's sin and before Bathsheba found out that she was pregnant. For several months David's unconfessed sin had played its role in David's heart. He had been spiritually defeated. Now David wanted once again the joy of salvation that he had with God in past days. Also, David was asking for the "generous Spirit," which was the Holy Spirit working in his heart.

Then David makes the promise, *"I will teach transgressors Your ways, and sinners shall be converted to You"* (Psalm 51:13 NKJV). We do not know if David ever attempted to go and lead sinners to repentance. Perhaps not individually, but as a leader of the people of God he fulfilled that role. But one way or another, David was determined to restore his right relationship with God. He determined to do what was necessary to renew God's work through him.

"Deliver me from the guilt of bloodshed" (Psalm 51:14 NKJV). David was deeply aware of his sin in plotting the murder against Uriah, even though he did not actually plunge the dagger into Uriah's body (2 Samuel 11). Yet David felt convicted of what he had done, and he knew he was guilty of the murder of Uriah. Therefore, he made special mention of this great sin

in his repentance. When David finally prayed to the "God of my salvation," surely he knew that his prayer would be answered.

David's forgiveness involved more than offering a sacrifice for his sin. Note that David prayed, *"You do not desire sacrifice, or else I would give it"* (Psalm 51:16 NKJV). David understood that forgiveness of sin was God's response to his heart, and it involved more than a "clean" heart. It involved regaining God's presence in his life. He prayed from the depth of his heart for forgiveness. How do we know that? Because David confessed, *"The sacrifices of God are a broken spirit, a broken and a contrite heart"* (Psalm 51:17 NKJV).

David's importance as a king is not mentioned in his prayer. His confession was not about David's wrong use of his power as king. David realized he had committed something worse than murder—he sinned against God Himself. He lost the presence of God in his life.

When David says "a broken spirit," he is using the Hebrew word to mean a broken pot or bottle, something that cannot be put together—except by God. So when you have a hard or stony heart, God can break it. Why? To bring you back to a place of seeking forgiveness and cleansing.

Did David get release? Notice he said, *"These, O God, You will not despise"* (Psalm 51:17 NKJV).

People reading this story may not understand David's heart. The king could do anything he wanted to—he could take women and commit adultery with them and get away with it. But not David, because his relationship to God was greater than any relationship with the people of his nation or even with Bathsheba herself.

David came straight to God knowing that God does not despise a broken and contrite heart.

CHAPTER 4

PSALM 84: PRAYING TO ENJOY GOD'S PRESENCE

I want you to enjoy coming into My presence in the tabernacle and expressing your deep passion for the courts of My house. May your flesh cry out when you are not there. The sparrows are so comfortable in My presence that they make their nest within sight of My altar. I want you to rest near My presence because I am your King and your God. I will bless those who linger in My house because they worship and praise Me, Selah! I will bless those who realize their strength is in Me because My principles direct their hearts. Worshipers come to Me through a valley of weeping; they fill pools with their tears. They continue climbing from strength to strength in their endeavor to find My peace. They desire to know Me, their Lord and God, and to look into My face, Selah! One day in My courts enjoying My presence is better than a thousand days anywhere else. Worshipers would rather be a doorkeeper in My house than live sumptuously in the tents of wickedness. I will shine warmth on their life like the sun; I will protect them like a shield. I will not withhold any good thing from them when they walk uprightly. Blessed are those who trust in Me.

—Psalm 84, author's paraphrase

Can you see David leaving his throne, walking out of the throne room, going northward out of the palace toward the Temple? Several court servants run up to remind David of different things he must do and different places he must be. But David does not pay attention to them. Even though there is a big banquet that night and they are waiting for David before they enter the banquet room, there is something else that attracts David and to which he devotes his life. It is the presence of God. So David continues his walk toward the Temple. Each evening there were prayers in the Temple around 4 p.m., and David wanted to be in the presence of God.

Some Bibles attribute Psalm 84 to the sons of Korah; however, certain Bibles attribute it to David. Spurgeon, the great pastor of the 1800s, said that this psalm had "Davidic perfume," meaning it smelled like David and carried the same pleasant aroma of David's psalms.

John Calvin also said, "In all probability David was its author." Even Martin Luther, the 1500s reformer, said that Psalm 84 speaks like David was the author.

The psalm begins by describing how expressively lovely and dear were the tabernacles full of the Lord. Here David uses the plural *tabernacles*, so was he referring to the Temple, or was he referring to certain side rooms in the Temple where he could go to pray and meet God?

Whatever David is describing, he does not even attempt to tell you what they are like. He just uses the plural wording of tabernacles, and many scholars have said it is a reference to the many subdivisions in God's Temple, each one having the presence of God.

When David prayed, *"My soul longeth, yea, even fainteth for the courts of the Lord"* (Psalm 84:2 KJV), he used the Hebrew word *kalah*, signifying a faint, when you are consumed by your surroundings and what is happening to you. Today somebody might say, "I am dying to visit the church sanctuary." David understood that even birds like sparrows and swallows were comfortable in God's house. Even for one small moment, David seemed to wish he was like the birds who could settle down in the house of God: *"Blessed are they that dwell in thy house"* (Psalm 84:4 KJV).

David describes the difficulty that one had climbing up to the top of Mount Zion to finally enter the Temple. That person would have to pass the well of Maca. We assume he was describing the valley of Bochim, which is mentioned in Judges 2:1 as the valley of mulberry trees (see 2 Samuel 5:23-24; 1 Chronicles 14:14-15).

The man who made this climb would never be without water to carry him from "strength to strength."

One traveling up to worship God finds that the difficulty of travel is measured by the promise of God's presence when arriving at the Temple. Therefore, the ultimate purpose is not the climb, or the success, but to enjoy the presence of God Himself. It's the purpose of worship that lures the traveler to do all that he can to find God's presence.

When the Bible talks about going from "strength to strength" it means we gain strength from meeting God in the house, and the more we meet Him the stronger we become to climb to new heights.

Why does David want to go to the top? He wants to *"look upon the face of thine anointed"* (Psalm 84:9 KJV).

Before the time of Jesus Christ, many would think that the phrase *"thine anointed"* was a reference to the anointed king of God's people. That would have been first David and later Solomon and those who followed. But as we read it through the eyes of the New Testament, we know that the Anointed One is Jesus Christ.

When David said that he wanted to "look upon the face of thine anointed," he was suggesting that His countenance would shine upon him and give him strength to make the continued effort to climb into the house of God.

And what was the goal? *"A day in thy courts is better than a thousand"* (Psalm 84:10 KJV).

In David's lifetime he enjoyed many seats of honor, at official banquets as well as unofficial gatherings when he would gather with his soldiers or others. But in his heart, David said, *"I would rather be a doorkeeper in the house of my God"* (Psalm 84:10 NKJV). That meant he would simply be a servant who would look after the comfort and welfare of those in God's tent. David, who is king of Israel and the top of all Israelites, is willing to be at the bottom—a servant—to enjoy the presence of God in His house.

David wanted to be a *doorkeeper*, which meant he was one of the lowest of servants. He was willing to be that low to get close to the Lord, rather than to live in the tents of the wicked.

David abruptly announced, *"The Lord God is a sun and shield"* (Psalm 84:11 NKJV). Again, David was speaking of both the warmth that comes from the sun and protection that comes from all attempts to kill him. And who would that be? God would be the sun to give him warmth and light, and God would be his protection to keep him from all danger and evil.

Also, by asking God to be a sun, he is asking God to direct his paths so that he can follow the Lord and accomplish his purpose. And as David follows the Lord and encounters trouble, the Lord is his shield—the One who preserves his going out and coming in.

But David knows it is more than just winning the battle: *"the Lord will give grace and glory"* (Psalm 84:11 NKJV). When you receive the free gift of God's grace, it secures the promise of Heaven's glory to come.

David concludes this psalm by promising, *"the Lord will give grace and glory: no good thing will he withhold from them that walk uprightly"* (Psalm 84:11 NKJV). That is a wonderful promise from the Lord of Hosts, and David trusted Him and you should trust Him too.

CHAPTER 5
PSALM 90: PRAYING THROUGH LIFE'S STRUGGLES

*I, the Lord, have been your dwelling place throughout all generations.
Before I created the mountains, even before I created the earth, even
from everlasting to everlasting, I am God. I determined that all people
will die, I decreed that you would all return to dust. A thousand years
in My sight is but yesterday that is gone; it's just a watch in the night.
I carry away your years like a flood, your life is like sleep after you
awake. Your life is like grass that springs up in the morning, you grow
throughout the day; in the evening you are cut down, then you wither
and die. My anger can consume you; My wrath brings you trouble.
I see all of your disobediences; I shine My light on your secret sins.
When I am angry with you, your life passes away quickly. Your simple
life does not amount to much, like a tale that someone tells. You live
approximately three score and ten years; some reach the golden age
of four score years. But they have physical difficulties and pain, then
their life is cut off and they fly away. No one knows when I am angry
at them, so you must always trust Me in fear. So, I will teach you to
make each day count, so that you can live wisely. I—the Lord God—
will shine My beauty upon you, I will establish the work of your
hands, yes, the work of your hands I will establish.*

—Psalm 90:1-12,17, author's paraphrase

Psalm 90 is a prayer of Moses to understand God, to seek His blessing and
fullness in the life of the one praying, and then to be able to live through
all of the punishment that is coming to them because they have sinned
against God and not done His will.

A few people have objected to Moses' authorship because he says the
average life of a person is 80 years, and we know that Moses lived to be

120 (see Deuteronomy 34:7). However, the Scriptures make a clear case that Moses' longevity is an exception. Even Caleb describes his 85 years as being an exception or out of the ordinary (see Joshua 14:10).

Moses begins this psalm reflecting on the past, reminding us that we have lived in God's presence, enjoyed God's goodness, and only have life because God has given us the time we live. *"Thou hast been our dwelling place in all generations"* (Psalm 90:1 KJV).

Quickly, Moses goes on to talk about the length of the earth in God's presence. He states, *"Before the mountains were brought forth...from everlasting to everlasting, thou art God"* (Psalm 90:2 KJV).

God was leading His people through the wilderness toward the Promised Land and a place where He would live with them in the Temple on top of Mount Zion. Yet Moses is saying there had never been a geographical locality for God; rather, the people always dwelt in Jehovah Himself: *"thou hast been our dwelling place"* (Psalm 90:1 KJV).

Moses writes, *"Before the mountains were brought forth"* (Psalm 90:2 KJV), suggesting that mountains might be the grandest and most ancient of all of God's creation. He created them in the beginning. Yet even when God created the world, He had a blueprint in mind so that the earth was a product of His creative fingers.

And remember when God was creating, He was gloriously present: *"from everlasting to everlasting, thou art God"* (Psalm 90:2 KJV).

Abruptly Moses writes, *"Thou turnest man to destruction"* (Psalm 90:3 KJV). Moses recognizes that the Almighty created Adam from the dust of the ground and made man into the first pattern for all that should follow him. Still, each person is frail in the presence of Almighty God. He who created the world with His spoken word has the power to bring man to destruction with His word.

Next, Moses moves on to time: *"For a thousand years in thy sight are but as yesterday when it is past"* (Psalm 90:4 KJV). God is omniscient, always knowing everything; God is omnipotent, always powerful to do anything He chooses; God is omnipresent, always present everywhere in the world He created. Again, "from everlasting to everlasting"—God has no lifeline, no beginning, and no end; He is the eternal God *"I Am that I Am"* (Exodus 3:14 KJV).

Again, look at the Person of God, *"For a thousand years in thy sight are but as yesterday when it is past"* (Psalm 90:4 KJV). That means God is above time. Before everything existed, God existed, and He will continue to exist after everything is passed away. God is eternal. Even the apostle Peter said, *"One day is with the Lord as a thousand years, and thousand years as one day"* (2 Peter 3:8 KJV).

Moses describes this as a "watch in the night." A watch in the night describes going to sleep and awaking the next morning; sleeping time means nothing. Just as sleep is from beginning to end, so the duration of man on the earth is from beginning to end.

Moses describes, *"Thou carriest them away as with a flood"* (Psalm 90:5 KJV). As a current of water rushes through a valley washing away everything in its path, so time rushes through humanity carrying all people in its tide. But God sees us in the flood, preserves us, uses us, indwells us, and then brings us into His presence at our death.

But let's discuss how God uses us. People are like grass that grows up early in the morning—it covers the meadows with the beauty of its blades of grass. The writer describes it, *"the morning it flourisheth, and groweth up"* (Psalm 90:6 KJV). But people are described as *"in the evening it is cut down, and withereth"* (Psalm 90:6 KJV). There is an old saying, "Old age and the coffin is covered with flowers of youth, both watching as we are buried beneath the earth."

The writer turns his attention from life in general to the condition of Israel after they sinned against God and were wandering in the wilderness, lost without a destination. Their only hope was in God Himself to give them eternal life after they pass. Then the psalmist says, *"For we are consumed by thine anger"* (Psalm 90:7 KJV). He is describing the punishment that God gave Israel for 40 years in the wilderness. Then he describes it further, *"by thy wrath are we troubled"* (Psalm 90:7 KJV). And why did God do that? *"Thou hast set our iniquities before thee"* (Psalm 90:8 KJV). In case any Israelite points to someone else who is a greater sinner than them, the psalmist reminds us, *"our secret sins in the light of thy countenance"* (Psalm 90:8 KJV).

In Egypt, Israel complained of the harsh taskmasters who beat them with whips to make them build the pyramids and monuments of Egypt.

But Israel was delivered from Egypt by God who carried them through the miracle of the Red Sea, provided manna from Heaven to feed them, and water to nourish them. But Israel did not learn the lessons they should have learned; they left the harsh taskmasters of Egypt to face the wrath of an angry God whom they would not obey. The people during Moses' day knew trouble. Here the psalmist describes them, *"We spend our years as a tale that is told"* (Psalm 90:9 KJV). The Hebrew language says, "we continue our years with a groan." The Hebrew word *kemo* is more than an expression of pain—it is groaning under oppression.

While some say life is sweet and swift, to the Israelites life was swift and not sweet, but was agonizing to the end. Most describe the duration of life as "three score and ten," i.e., 70 years old. Moses died at the age of 120 (see Deuteronomy 34:7); Aaron died at the age of 123 (see Numbers 33:39). These brothers were the exception to the case, but most people are fortunate to live to 70 years and sometimes beyond. But even then, the Bible describes their life as "labor and sorrow," and before you know it your life flies away.

So what does Moses do with the briefness of life? He gives them a prayer. *"Teach us to number our days, that we may apply our hearts unto wisdom"* (Psalm 90:12 KJV). That is what the reader of this book should pray.

When speaking about wanting longevity of life, Moses immediately returns to praying, *"Return, O Lord, how long?"* (Psalm 90:13 KJV). Moses is asking how long before God turns His anger into acceptance and mercy. Here Moses is praying, *"let it repent thee concerning thy servants"* (Psalm 90:13 KJV). Moses is asking God to repent of what He is going to do in punishing His people. Then Moses gives a description of that good life, *"satisfy us early with thy mercy; that we may rejoice and be glad all our days"* (Psalm 90:14 KJV). That is a prayer that God would fulfill His purpose for us—the joy of living out life with God's presence and blessing and not spending all our time in sorrow.

Next, Moses says that the work of God would be the source of their joy and reward. *"Let thy work appear unto thy servants, and thy glory unto their children"* (Psalm 90:16 KJV). Here Moses is praying that God's glory will show to His children and to each succeeding generation. The psalmist is praying for the establishment of Israel in the Promised Land and each generation enjoying its fruit and the presence of God.

Moses ends his prayer by saying, *"Let the beauty of the Lord our God be upon us"* (Psalm 90:17 KJV). Interesting prayer; Moses and his generation would not see the Promised Land. But they wanted to see the beauty of the Holy Land and enjoy its pleasant fruit.

His final prayer is, *"establish thou the work of our hands"* (Psalm 90:17 KJV). He is asking for his influence to live through his children and the next generation.

Chapter 6

Psalm 100: Rejoicing as You Enter God's Presence

Lord, I shout with joy to You; everyone from every nation joins me. I worship as I enter Your presence with singing because You, Lord, are my God. You made us and we belong to You; we are Your people and the sheep of Your pasture. Lord, I come into Your gates giving thanks; I enter the courts with praise. I bless Your holy name by giving thanks for all You've done for me. Lord, You are good, Your mercy is everlasting, and Your truth endures forever.

—Psalm 100 ELT

This psalm has a simple title, *a psalm of thanksgiving*, and is the only psalm that has this title. Therefore, it is a psalm of invitation inviting you, but not just you, the whole earth to come and worship the Lord with thanksgiving. It is a psalm with jubilant confidence that the whole earth will come to worship Him. It is a picture of the future glory when all people submit to the reign of the Lord God and worship Him completely with all their hearts.

Worshiping with all the heart is something that usually does not happen with a group, or as an individual. But in the future you shall worship God completely, more than any time on this earth, because when you no longer have a sin nature, you will be able to know God perfectly and worship Him perfectly. But not only you, all saved people will submit to the reign of the Lord and worship Him.

The New King James Version of the Bible translates it, "Make a joyful *shout* to the Lord." The King James says, "make a joyful *noise*." Noise is just a loud sound or loud distraction to your heart. But make a joyful *shout* to the Lord is something you do with the force of your mind, the intent of your will, and the obedience of your vocal chords and mouth. You make a decision to shout because of who He is and what He has done for you.

A joyful shout reflects the glad and extreme verbal response that loyal subjects give to the king when he appears before his subjects. Since God is a happy God, He should be worshiped by happy people; therefore, make a joyful noise. And what is that? It is the equivalent of your worship, homage, or recognizing the greatness and power of the King.

When we see the phrase "*all you lands,*" this means that all nations must recognize who the Lord is. He is Yahweh, Jehovah, and because of His grace and mercy each person exists.

The phrase "*serve the Lord with gladness*" is a reference to those who come into the Temple to worship God in the Old Testament, or we who go into God's presence in the New Testament to worship Him. This principle of worshiping God with all our hearts applies to any service we give to God; we are to "serve the Lord" with all our hearts and do it with gladness.

This psalm is about happiness. It is our duty and privilege to be happy as we worship God. God intended that our worship to Him would remove human misery and disappointment and all the sorrows tied to the failure of mankind. An old scholar once said, "If your religion does not make you happy, you do not understand your religion, nor do you understand the One who gives it to you."

This psalm commands us to "serve the Lord." We do serve the Lord because we love Him and it is our delight to worship Him in service. When the psalm tells us, "*Come before His presence with singing,*" as it does throughout the book of Psalms, our praise is expressed in singing or music. Singing is not the only way to praise the Lord, but is one of the quick ways we can do it.

And why do we praise God? Because we "*know that the Lord, He is God.*" When we recognize His true deity and all of His power, we cannot do anything but praise Him. And when we know God, we have a sure foundation for worshiping God and thanking Him for all He has done for us.

Yet there is another reason we should worship God: "*It is He who has made us.*" Since He originally made Adam and Eve and we are eventually children from that first couple, then we should praise God for the life we have and the opportunity to serve God. It is absolutely ridiculous to think that we could make ourselves or that we could be as we are by our own efforts. Therefore, we should worship the One who has created us and made us who we are.

And that brings us to God's proprietorship. That means He owns us and has all rights over us. Understand that we can fully give Him our total love and adoration. Yet because we are born again, the believer has a new and greater reason for praising God. They not only are born as a human created by God, but now they are a new creature created in Christ Jesus (see 2 Corinthians 5:17). We have new life in Jesus because we have His life.

Yet there is another reason we worship God. It is because He has chosen us as His people, and He cares for us like a shepherd cares for His sheep. Remember the shepherd owns the sheep, cares for the sheep, and will give his life for his sheep. Why? Because the sheep are his life, and his life exists through his sheep.

There is another reason we should praise Him. *"We are the sheep of His pasture."* Notice the phrase "His pasture." This world is not our home—it belongs to God and we live in His world and magnify Him in His house.

THE WHAT AND WHY OF WORSHIP

Therefore, if you are a child of God, you ought to come into His house with thanks and praise. *"Enter into His gates with thanksgiving, and into His courts with praise."* The phrase "entering his gates and courts" conveys to us how we should mentally approach God. We are coming into His presence, not inviting God to come into our world. We come humbly, thankfully, and worshipfully. And how do we worship? With thanksgiving.

We must learn early that our role of praising and thanking and worshiping God is more than our private expression. We join with other people and want to come with them because they know the Lord. We join with other people to worship and praise the Lord together. Remember, worship is never private; it begins in the privacy of your mind, but it never stops there. When you come to worship God, you come with all of His people worshiping God together.

WHY WORSHIP?

We worship the Lord *"for the Lord is good."* So when you come offering praise and worship to God, you recognize His goodness in all that He has done for you—giving you the right to come to Him, forgiving you of your sins, and accepting you based on the blood of His Son Jesus Christ.

The gods of the heathen were not good gods; they were selfish and they turned against the people to hurt them or destroy them.

But not our God—He is a good God. *"His mercy is everlasting."* And how long is everlasting? Forever and ever. It does not cease, but will always exist.

One day we shall behold the everlasting gates of Heaven and enter into the home of God. It is then that we will see God, praise God, and worship Him in His holiness.

THREE MAIN POINTS

There are three main ideas in Psalm 100. First, the psalmist wants you to know that the Lord is God, and He is a great and powerful God who has created mankind. God is also a good God who has given good things to us.

Second, the psalmist wants you to know that we are the sheep of God and we live in His pasture, and God will take care of us.

Third, the psalmist wants you to realize God is good. Therefore, when you come to worship Him, it is appropriate to turn up the volume. Notice what you can do when you worship God. You can shout your worship; you enter His presence to praise and bless His holy name. But it all ends up in worship. When you obey all of God's commandments, you come singing to God, and shouldn't you sing at the top of your voice with all that is within you? Yet there are times you sing softly because when you whisper your praise to God, it comes from the quietness of your soul and tells God that He is the only thing that exists in your world.

In Psalm 100, God appears as the divine Creator who brought His people into existence and gave them life so they could worship Him, praise Him, and obey Him. They owe their self-identity to God who is their Creator.

Psalm 100 gives us two images of the Lord. First, He is the Shepherd who looks after us and cares for us. We are the "sheep of His pasture." The second image is that God is the King. So we enter into the city of the King through "His gates," finally ending up in His "courts." And when we arrive there we give praise, thanksgiving, and worship Him, blessing His name.

Remember, praise moves you from outside of God's city into God's presence, through His gates, and into His courts, so you come into His very presence where you praise His holy name because the Lord is good. What are you doing? You are worshiping Him.

The word *good* (*tob*) is the Hebrew word reflecting God's purity in nature and actions and in His continued relationship with us.

When you sing and praise God with the words of Psalm 100, you join a vast community of worshipers throughout history who have praised God for His goodness and all that He has done for us.

CHAPTER 7

PSALM 102: PRAYING WHEN OVERWHELMED WITH GRIEF

Lord, listen to me and hear me when I request help for my troubles. Answer me quickly and don't turn away because I hurt all the time and my life is disappearing like smoke. I've lost my appetite to eat anything, and I am reduced to just skin and bones.

I am like a lonely owl or sparrow that's lost in the desert, and I cannot sleep.

My enemies are always criticizing and cursing me, destroying my reputation. I have lost my appetite to eat and my tears fill up a glass. You Lord have cast me aside and You punish me in Your anger. My future is a black shadow, and I am drying up like cut grass.

But You Lord live forever and will be known in coming generations. You will show Your love and favor on Jerusalem and will restore Your city in the future. You love the stones that were used to build Jerusalem and even the dirt on which it was built. Leaders of nations that hate Jerusalem will see Your protection for the city and will tremble. You will demonstrate Your glory by rebuilding Jerusalem and ultimately answer the prayers of its protectors who have been attacked and defeated.

—Psalm 102:1-17 ELT

This is a psalm that describes the writer's afflictions, how he is overwhelmed with grief and problems. But it is also a messianic psalm that describes all the trials and pain endured by Jesus the Messiah. Note in this psalm there is no musical notation that directs the reader to chant or sing; rather, it should be read in private to understand the grief that the Messiah suffered.

Some feel this was written after the return of Ezra and the remnant of Israel to the Promised Land with God's command to rebuild the Temple (see Nehemiah 1:3-11). Also, some have suggested this psalm was written by Jeremiah or Daniel as they looked at the sufferings of the nation of Israel, projecting toward the sufferings of the Messiah. Others feel it was written by David and was entirely prophetic, speaking of the sufferings of Jesus Christ.

The message of verses 25-27 predicts the coming of Messiah:

Of old hast thou laid the foundation of the earth: and the heavens are the work of thy hands. They shall perish, but thou shalt endure: yea, all of them shall wax old like a garment; as a vesture shalt thou change them, and they shall be changed: but thou art the same, and thy years shall have no end (Psalm 102:25-27 KJV).

Psalm 102 is quoted in Hebrews 1:10-12 demonstrating its messianic prediction:

You, Lord, in the beginning laid the foundation of the earth, and the heavens are the work of Your hands. They will perish, but You remain; and they will all grow old like a garment; like a cloak You will fold them up, and they will be changed. But You are the same; and Your years will not fail (Hebrews 1:10-12 NKJV).

Charles Spurgeon says this prayer toward Heaven with its mourning and grief is the result of the psalmist being afflicted or suffering. This psalmist is more concerned about the extent of his suffering than he is about the words that he prays or the relief he seeks. Technically, there are few formal petitions in this prayer, but there is a steady stream of supplication from beginning to end about the difficulties he is enduring.

The psalmist is primarily concerned with his own suffering, but also with others who are being afflicted—for Jerusalem and Zion and the house of the Lord. Note his love for his hometown: "*For your people love every stone in her walls and cherish even the dust in her streets*" (Psalm 102:14 NLT). This psalm is a picture of a cup that has been filled with grief and suffering, then turned upside down so that everything in his heart is poured out from his great trouble in his plea for God to help and deliver him.

This psalmist is not complaining, nor is he trying to find fault or accusing those who harm him; rather he is "moaning" an expression of pain, not rebellion but an honest confession. He is faithful to the Lord and Jerusalem, so this psalm could be called the *patriot's lament*.

His complaints do not represent one who has no hope; rather, he has faith in God and looks for God to not only save him but resurrect the nation of Israel and again show favor to Jerusalem and the Temple: "*For the Lord will rebuild Jerusalem. He will appear in his glory*" (Psalm 102:16 NLT).

The psalmist is not content with just praying for the sake of talking to God; he really desires to reach the ear and heart of his God. His prayer is not telling others about his problem, but when he talks to God he knows God is hearing and listening and He will answer in due time.

As you read the introduction to Psalm 102, you feel the great earnestness and urgency of the psalmist to pray.

> *Hear my prayer, O Lord, and let my cry come unto thee. Hide not thy face from me in the day when I am in trouble; incline thine ear unto me: in the day when I call answer me speedily* (Psalm 102:1-2 KJV).

These phrases *hear, cry, hide not, I am in trouble, incline thine ear, call,* and *speedily* show how earnestly and sincerely the psalmist is praying.

When the psalmist prays, "*hide not thy face from me*" (Psalm 102:2 KJV), he is asking for access to the presence of God. He wants to enjoy the presence of God and feel His approval. What is the psalmist saying? "I can bear my difficulties, but now in my heavy distress, I want the favor of God's presence and compassion."

When the psalmist prays, "*incline Your to me*" (Psalm 102:2 NKJV), is it because God had turned His face away? When the psalmist could not see the face of God, at least he wanted the ear of God to listen to his prayers. Have you ever felt you just had a side view of God—you had His ear? If so, at least you can pray, "Lend me Your ear"—that is when God bends down to listen.

When the psalmist prays, "*answer me speedily*" he is asking God to respond to his prayer as soon as possible. He doesn't even wonder if it would be wise for the Lord to delay His answer. No! The psalmist's importunity captures the moment. He wants an answer, and he wants it now! And why does he want it now?

> *For my days disappear like smoke, and my bones burn like red-hot coals. My heart is sick, withered like grass, and I have lost my appetite. Because of my groaning, I am reduced to skin and bones. I am like an owl in the desert, like a little owl in a far-off wilderness. I lie awake, lonely as a solitary bird on the roof* (Psalm 102:3-7 NLT).

When the psalmist said his days "*disappear like smoke*," he was confessing to the emptiness of his life. His actions were meaningless, and his time was passing away into nothingness. When the psalmist said, "*my bones burn like red-hot coals*," he was describing a firebrand taken from a roaring fire and used elsewhere to start another fire. The psalmist was describing his life like one who is carrying a message to those who would read his words.

Next the psalmist describes himself as "*withered like grass*" (Psalm 102:4 NLT). Just as a plant is parched by the extreme heat of the noonday sun and is about to die, so the psalmist says he is wilted and the sun is burning up all of his energy. His life and its beauty are dwindling, he has no joy, and the freshness of life is being wasted by his anguish.

Now, the psalmist sees himself as an emaciated body and he is reduced to a living skeleton. He cries out "*my bones cleave to my skin*" (Psalm 102:5 KJV). That distress motivates him to be in Zion, to enter the tabernacle, and to be refreshed by the presence of God.

In the next few verses, the psalmist describes himself with three birds, each one described in isolation. He sees himself as a lone solider keeping guard for the Lord. He complains that others are too selfish to help him, or too careless to care. He is like a bird that sits on the rooftop alone, miserable, sitting by himself.

First, the *pelican* is an interesting term because from its Hebrew root *quat* comes the verb "to vomit." That perhaps is because the pelican grabs food in its large bill and then carries it to her young. Then the pelican regurgitates food for the young pelicans to eat. Hence the word for pelican is to *vomit*. Is the psalmist saying that he is like a pelican that has taken in the message of God—like food—and will ultimately vomit it out of his mouth?

Next he describes himself as an owl, which is known for inhabiting isolated places in the desert. Finally, he describes himself like a sparrow, perhaps because it is the weakest and smallest of all the birds and is a picture of the solitude of the psalmist as he sees himself weak and isolated from help. Perhaps he is using these words to describe his awful loneliness as a messianic reference to the loneliness of Jesus Christ as He was facing the judgment of the cross.

Not only is the psalmist concerned about his lack of fellowship with God's people, he speaks about *"Mine enemies reproach me all the day"* (Psalm 102:8 KJV)—again, a reference to the Messiah. Can you hear the despair in his voice and his anger because no one is with him? It is a description of tremendous anger against the persecution of Jesus Christ, perhaps greater than any natural anger because it was satanically inspired against the Son of God who was sinless and pure.

And what does the psalmist say? *"They are mad against me."* When his enemies attack him, it cuts like a razor and he feels it is repeated all day, every day. Isn't that a description of those who demanded the crucifixion of Jesus Christ when they cried out "crucify Him, crucify Him"? They did it without reason or cause. They did it because of the evil in their hearts inspired by satan.

When the psalmist describes, *"I have eaten ashes like bread"* (Psalm 102:9 NKJV), he is describing fasting. During a fast, many would throw ashes on their heads to demonstrate grief to God. It goes beyond ashes to eat—think about tears in the cup one is drinking. He is describing an all-saturating and all-embedded sadness.

This describes Jesus Christ, demonstrating the great destress and humiliation of the cross. But it was more than the wrath of man—the death of Christ also was a picture of the wrath of God: *"because of thine indignation and thy wrath"* (Psalm 102:10 KJV). Yes, the people hated Jesus Christ and crucified Him. But a greater picture is seen of Jesus carrying the sin of the world, when all sin was punished and judged by God the Father: *"For He [God the Father] made Him [God the Son] who knew no sin to be sin for us, that we might become the righteousness of God in Him"* (2 Corinthians 5:21 NKJV).

Finally, without friends, an enemy angry against him having sworn an oath to destroy him, the psalmist cries out to God. He now turns to God and describes the will of the Lord in his pain. *"Because of thine indignation and thy wrath"* (Psalm 102:10 KJV). He has a sense of divine wrath that is causing his pain. Some feel that this is a reference to when God takes His presence and protection away from Israel and God sends Babylon to conquer the Promised Land and takes Israel away as slaves across the Euphrates River.

The phrase *"lifted me up, and cast me down"* (Psalm 102:10 KJV) is a picture of a boat that is being pummeled by a hurricane and fierce winds. That is how the psalmist sees his life, and that is an expression of the helplessness he is feeling. All the violence in his life is leading to a desperate fall. The psalmist is depicting the overpowering terror that carries him along, and he does not know where he is going or what lies ahead.

The psalmist describes, *"My days are like a shadow that declineth"* (Psalm 102:11 KJV). As an old man his shadow is declining, predicting his end is coming and is nearby. The shadow is an unstable picture of life, so how terrible it must be to see your life as a declining shadow. The psalmist uses this threatening picture to express how terrible his condition.

Next, he describes himself, *"I am withered like grass"* (Psalm 102:11 KJV). Here is a picture of the hot sun parching the green grass. Finally, the grass is cut down with a scythe and dries out in the burning sun. The psalmist feels as though his life is going from him and his strength is leaving until he dies. Our flesh is best described as grass when it is cut down— just as grass fades, its beauty passes, it dries up, and then it dies.

As you read Psalm 102, there is an abrupt change from the first section, verses 1-11, to verses 12-14. Why this abrupt change? The psalmist—inspired by God—is changing from his focus on Messiah's sufferings to his focus on God's people in Jerusalem. This shows a picture of God's readiness to help both the city of Zion and Messiah. When he writes, *"but thou, O Lord, shall endure for ever"* (Psalm 102:12 KJV), the context seems to suggest he is talking about God the Father continuing His relationship with His people, the Jews in Jerusalem. But we cannot escape the fact that it is also a reference to Jesus the Messiah.

The psalmist turns away from his personal troubles to see the strength and beauty of the Lord. *"You, O Lord, shall endure forever"* (Psalm102:12 NKJV). The word *endure* in the Hebrew language is for the word *sit,* suggesting that Jehovah will sit in eternity to see all that is going on, and He will reign on His throne with a purpose for us and for our life. It is that vision of God that gives him hope and a purpose for life. The psalmist is saying, "I perish, but Lord, You will endure forever." And so the writer is describing his nation, saying, "My nation has almost become extinct like dead grass, but You, Lord, are all together unchanged and eternal."

The security of God in Heaven is an anchor for those who are drifting— the Lord rules and reigns, whatever happens.

The phrase *"endure forever"* reminds us that God exists now, He will always exist, and He always has existed in the past. What God was in the Old Testament to Israel, He will be to us today, and He will be to His people in the future.

Let us confirm to our children all that God is so they can pass on to their children a hope in God that they too will follow Him as we have followed.

Why does the psalmist write, *"thy remembrance unto all generations"* (Psalm 102:12 KJV)? It is because time is in God's control. Immediately he says, *"for the time to favour her, yea, the set time, is come"* (Psalm 102:13 KJV). Technically, the psalmist is referring to the time for restoring the city of Jerusalem after it is destroyed by Babylon in 587 BC. Throughout Scripture, the desolation and judgment on the city of Jerusalem is also a reference to the desolation on God's people because they have sinned. Just as the city of Jerusalem represented the sin of the Jews in the Old Testament, so God is forced to judge the people just as He did the city of Jerusalem.

As things are vanishing like smoke and so much of life is withering like grass, let's remember the one eternal, unchangeable truth that shines day after day—God sits upon His throne, knows our troubles, cares for us, and He will hear us when we cry out to Him. The psalmist prayed, *"Thou shalt arise, and have mercy upon Zion"* (Psalm 102:13 KJV). God will not always leave His people in a low condition. He may be hidden from our view at times, and we may think that we cannot see God; but in time He will return, He will defend us, He will work all things for His glory (see Romans 8:28).

God has a set time which He knows, but we do not know. At that set time God will expand the boundaries of His Kingdom and it will be God who will do the work in us, through us, and He will arise to do it.

Today we all pray what the psalmist prayed: *"So the heathen shall fear the name of the Lord"* (Psalm 102:15 KJV). Just as a light turned on in a house will shine out through its windows, so when Jesus who is the light of the world comes into the church and is magnified and obeyed, His light will shine through the windows of the church out into a dark world. It is then that the unsaved will see the power of the Lord, what He does in human lives, and how He can make a difference in all situations.

The future belongs to God, and His promise in this Psalm is: *"When the Lord shall build up Zion, he shall appear in his glory"* (Psalm 102:16 KJV). The prophetic psalmist is writing about a reconstruction yet not accomplished. He is predicting the day when the Lord shall once again restore the city of Jerusalem to its original and rightful place. But it is also predicting once again when the Messiah shall come, return to earth, and build His millennial Kingdom in Israel/Palestine, with Jerusalem as the capital.

Take confidence—what God has predicted for the nation will happen. In the same way, what God has predicted for you will happen. God has predicted that in this life we shall grow old and eventually die. But one day we shall live with Him in Heaven, and our new body will enjoy a new place:

> *In My Father's house are many mansions; if it were not so, I would have told you. I go to prepare a place for you. And if I go and prepare a place for you, I will come again and receive you to Myself; that where I am, there you may be also* (John 14:2-3 NKJV).

CHAPTER 8

PSALM 137: PRAYING, CRYING, SINGING, DREAMING

My people sat by the rivers of Babylon and wept when they remem-
bered Zion. They refused to sing joyfully, hanging their harps on
willow trees. Their captors demanded that they sing; those who impris-
oned them wanted entertainment, asking, "Sing us a song of Zion."
My people couldn't sing while being held captive in a strange land.
My people said they couldn't forget Jerusalem just as their right hand
couldn't forget its movement. My people said their tongue would stick
in their mouth if they did not remember Me, their Lord.

—Psalm 137:1-6, author's paraphrase

Human beings are made up of all types of emotions, and these feelings
run the gamut from extreme negative emotions that drain both body and
soul to positive emotions that make us sing, rejoice, and dream, which this
psalm makes us reach. Psalm 137 is one of the shortest of all of the psalms,
and yet in this brief glimpse into the human makeup, we see the vast difference between laughing and crying.

Think of the experiences that lead to the many different emotions.
What makes you cry? Sometimes you are lonely, you have been left des-
titute, and no one will help you. Sometimes loneliness comes out of your
despair from loss of dreams, loss of hope, and loss of future.

On the other hand there is laugher, all types of joy, and all kinds of
energy in human laughter. Laughter is an enjoyable expression of our
inner person. You may laugh at a joke or something you think is unusual
or unexpected, or you may even laugh at something that was extremely
humorous.

This short psalm describes Israel in captivity in Babylon and what the
Jewish people experienced there.

Scholars have found the Syriac version of this psalm was ascribed to David. But remember, David lived long before Israel ever went into captivity in Babylon. Therefore, we have to conclude that either David did not write this psalm and someone else wrote it and over a period of time the real author was lost, or it is possible that David could have written prophetically, dreaming of the future when Israel was going to be judged and sent into captivity in Babylon.

Therefore, the question is whether this psalm was written prophetically before the exile or historically after the exile.

The psalm begins with personal weeping by the author as he remembers being taken as a prisoner to Babylon. While there, he could not sing the joyful songs of Israel because they were captives. In a burst of grief, Israel determined they could not sing. Even when the enemy was guarding them and asked for songs, they admitted they could not sing.

When the psalmist speaks about willow trees (see Psalm 137:2), he is either referring to the Euphrates or the Tigris River or perhaps one of the canals that crisscross Babylon between those two rivers.

The picture here is of the captives from Israel in the land of the Tigris and Euphrates who were asked to entertain their guards. This evolving picture shows the grief of Israel, but in a play on emotions it portrays the true love of Israel for God and their home.

This psalm can be applied by any reader to things, places, or times in their life when they find themselves in negative situations. But the psalmist is telling the reader to look within their memory to other times and other places where they enjoyed life. The point is, "Think back to times in your past when you enjoyed life, and let that memory carry you through your personal difficulty."

Therefore, learn that the memory of your past has power—power to heal, power to encourage, power to help you face the future.

The key to Psalm 137 is found in the last word in the text—*Lord*. The key to present happiness and joy is the Lord, and in the same way the key to surviving a hurtful past is also the Lord. The key to living in a hurtful present is knowing the joys of the Lord in the past. He is also available for the present and the future.

CHAPTER 9
PSALM 139: THANKSGIVING FOR GOD'S PRESENCE

O Lord, thou hast searched me, and known me. Thou knowest my downsitting and mine uprising, thou understandest my thought afar off. Thou compassest my path and my lying down, and art acquainted with all my ways. For there is not a word in my tongue, but, lo, O Lord, thou knowest it altogether. Thou hast beset me behind and before, and laid thine hand upon me. Such knowledge is too wonderful for me; it is high, I cannot attain unto it. Whither shall I go from thy spirit? or whither shall I flee from thy presence? If I ascend up into heaven, thou art there: if I make my bed in hell, behold, thou art there. If I take the wings of the morning, and dwell in the uttermost parts of the sea; Even there shall thy hand lead me, and thy right hand shall hold me. If I say, Surely the darkness shall cover me; even the night shall be light about me. Yea, the darkness hideth not from thee; but the night shineth as the day: the darkness and the light are both alike to thee. For thou hast possessed my reins: thou hast covered me in my mother's womb. I will praise thee; for I am fearfully and wonderfully made: marvellous are thy works; and that my soul knoweth right well. My substance was not hid from thee, when I was made in secret, and curiously wrought in the lowest parts of the earth. Thine eyes did see my substance, yet being unperfect; and in thy book all my members were written, which in continuance were fashioned, when as yet there was none of them. How precious also are thy thoughts unto me, O God! how great is the sum of them! If I should count them, they are more in number than the sand: when I awake, I am still with thee.

—Psalm 139:1-18 KJV

Psalm 139, ascribed to David, has been called one of the most beautiful of all the psalms in the Bible. And why is it beautiful? Because it describes God who does many wonderful things in a beautiful way, all for His glory, which is beautiful. His working with man is supernatural and therefore beautiful.

Of all of the psalms, it describes the omniscience, omnipotence, and omnipresence of God.

The thought of the psalm begins with "searching"—David says that the Lord has searched him and knows him. Then at the end David concludes with a prayer to God asking Him to *"Search me, O God, and know my heart; try me, and know my anxieties; and see if there is any wicked way in me, and lead me in the way everlasting"* (Psalm 139:23-24 NKJV).

David knew God and knew His heart perhaps better than anyone living during his lifetime. He address the "all-knowing God."

The first time he uses the word *search* (*chagar* in the original language), it means to dig as though one is digging for precious metal. So David is asking God to dig into his life and find the pure gold that is there in his walk before God. At the end of this psalm, David is praying for God to examine him. And what does he say about God who is going to examine him? God is omnipotent, omniscient, and omnipresent, so God can search him better than any person on earth. God can search him perfectly.

The word *search* is something we must do to God's Word—we must search the Scriptures to know them and how to live for God. When we search the Scriptures, we will find Him in the Bible. As we search God, we discover Him to know Him, find His plan for our lives, and obey Him. But at the same time God knows all things, so He knows us when He searches us. As a matter of fact, David testifies that every move he makes is known by God, seen by God, and measured by God. God even understands our thoughts "afar off." What does that mean? God knows our thoughts even before we think them. Even as our thoughts are forming in our mind, God knows what we are thinking.

Then next David says, *"Thou compassest my path and my lying down"* (Psalm 139:3 KJV). The word *compassest* is *zarah*, which means to sift grain to take out the chaff and get the good seed. That means God can go through all of our minds, see that which is chaff and throw it away, but

He is looking for the good seed in our minds. God is so intimately aware of all of our thoughts and actions that He sifts to know us inwardly and outwardly.

Next David confesses that, *"For there is not a word in my tongue, but, lo, O Lord, thou knowest it altogether"* (Psalm 139:4 KJV). Since God omnisciently knows our thoughts even before we begin to develop them in our mind, He knows how we think. We put words to our thoughts, followed by actions.

Next David says, *"Thou hast beset me behind and before"* (Psalm 139:5 KJV). When it comes to our past, God has recorded all of our thoughts and words, including our sins, but in His grace He blocks them out and applies the blood to cleanse us from all sin. He knows our thoughts before we do. So what does that mean? We cannot escape Him. God is behind us, He is in front of us, He is within us. As Charles Spurgeon said, we cannot outmarch God.

When David is told about the omniscience and omnipresence of God, he humbly admits, *"Such knowledge is too wonderful for me; it is high, I cannot attain unto it"* (Psalm 139:6 KJV). The fact that God knows everything about us even before we think it surpasses our comprehension of who God is. We worship Him for His greatness, but we really do not understand just how great He is. The knowledge that God has should comfort us, but it should also concern us that if we think of sin or are tempted to sin, God knows it even before we think or act.

Because of God's great omniscience, next David is overwhelmed by the omnipresence of God. *"Whither shall I go from thy spirit? or whither shall I flee from thy presence?"* (Psalm 139:7 KJV). David understands God's greatness of knowledge; now he is overwhelmed by God's presence. God is everywhere present always equally at the same time.

A man once asked a Christian, "Where is God?" The wise Christian was able to respond to the question by asking a question himself, "Let me first ask you, where is God not?"

Then the psalmist wants to know where he can go to flee from God's presence. Does this not remind us of when God called Jonah to go to Nineveh and preach to the lost in that city? It is then that Jonah ran from the presence of God, refusing to serve the Lord. So where can you go to flee from God? You cannot.

The psalmist said, *"If I ascend up into heaven, thou art there: if I make my bed in hell, behold, thou art there"* (Psalm 139:8 KJV). No one can escape the divine presence of God. You cannot run from God into Heaven nor can you flee from Him in hell. David found out why: *"Thou art there"* (Psalm 139:8 KJV).

David said, *"If I take the wings of the morning"* (Psalm 139:9 KJV). Perhaps that is a metaphor for the sunbeams that come from the early morning sun.

David was unable to escape the presence of God on this earth. Nowhere on the earth or in the sea could he hide from God.

David is unable to escape the presence of God, so he looks to hide in the darkness. Those people who try to hide in places where they cannot be seen think that if they cannot see in the dark place, no one can see them there. That is the expression of the psalmist.

But the psalm quickly reminds you that even the night, the darkness, shall be light when you try to hide from God. Why is that? Because darkness cannot hide from God; He is light. His light is brighter than the darkness. Then he says, *"the darkness and the light are both alike to thee"* (Psalm 139:12 KJV).

In verse 13 it moves into the omnipresence, the all-powerful energy of God: *"thou hast covered me in my mother's womb."* First, David addressed the omniscience of God (Psalm 139:1-6), then the omnipresence of God (Psalm 139:7-12). Now he moves into the all-powerful might and strength of God Almighty.

But when David says, *"For thou hast possessed my reins"* (Psalm 139:13 KJV), he uses a Hebrew word for the seat of emotions or sensation, i.e., feelings. This is the source of our desires and longing. The word for *reins* is *kilyah*, which means the kidney within the body. But poetically we refer to it as the inner nature of the human. So what does that mean? God knows and has power over the inner person, the desires, and longings.

When David says, *"I am fearfully and wonderfully made"* (Psalm 139:14 KJV), he describes God not only as putting the human body parts together, but weaving them as one would weave cloth or as one would weave a basket. We have the weaving of bones, tissues, organs, and the unborn are all under the control and guidance of God.

Let's not misunderstand. David says, "for I am fearfully and wonderfully made." The human body is so wonderful and fearful that those who study all aspects of the human anatomy stand in awe of the intricacy and precision of how the human body works together.

Next David describes, *"My substance was not hid from thee, when I was made in secret, and curiously wrought in the lowest parts of the earth"* (Psalm 139:15 KJV). As you look at the human body, much of what is there is hidden from the human eye, but God not only sees every inner part of the body, but He originally planned them, put them together, and guided everyone into their final existence in the womb of the mother. That includes everyone, including you and me.

Charles Spurgeon over a hundred years ago said, "Even so did the Lord fashion us when no eye beheld us, and the veil was not lifted til every member was complete." That means every part of the human body—veins, muscles, nerves, blood, organs—was embroidered together by God with great skill long before the world got its first look at us.

David said, *"Thine eyes did see my substance"* (Psalm 139:16 KJV). The Hebrew word *golen* for "substance" actually means anything that is rolled together in a ball, wrapped and held together by itself.

David is saying that the omnipotence and omnipresence of God actually guided the very formation of life in the womb, and yet that imperfect and unformed embryonic mass had life and would grow into a baby who was born in due time.

David uses an unusual expression, *"all my members were written, which in continuance were fashioned, when as yet there was none of them"* (Psalm 139:16 KJV). Here the omniscience of God, who knows all things, is putting together a human in the womb by the omnipotence of God, who can do all things, and even there in the womb is His omnipresence.

When you think of what God is doing in the womb, that is precious. Then David adds, *"How precious also are thy thoughts unto me, O God!"* (Psalm 139:17 KJV). The word *precious* means outstanding, irreplaceable. Anything that is precious is part of you, identifies you, and gives life and direction to your being.

In a day when a woman will give her body for an abortion to take the unborn baby's life, we who are Christians know that that unborn life has a soul, a soul that will live forever. Therefore, we reject abortion in any and all of its forms. Any life that is formed in the womb of a mother should be given an opportunity to live a life outside of the womb to the glory of God. At the same time, we understand that any baby who dies before the age of accountability will go into the presence of God.

"How precious also are thy thoughts unto me, O God!" (Psalm 139:17 KJV). If the forming of the baby in the womb is precious, how much more precious is the blueprint of God's plan where He formed life and brings it into existence.

When David says, *"how great is the sum of them"* (Psalm 139:17 KJV), he is saying if we could put them all together they would be immeasurable. *"If I should count them, they are more in number than the sand"* (Psalm 139:18 KJV).

Suddenly David changes his mood and direction. He speaks of God as "slaying the wicked" (see Psalm 139:19). Why is he concerned about the wicked? He calls them, "those that hate thee" (see Psalm 139:21). Those people grieve David and oppose David for who he is and what he believes and how he acts. He doesn't just hate them, he hates with *"perfect hatred"* (Psalm 139:22). This suggests that David not only was disgusted and nauseated by those who lifted their hand against God, he hated them as his enemies.

David began Psalm 139 with the statement that God had searched him; now he ends it with a prayer to God that God would *"search me, O God"* (Psalm 139:23). He wants God to know more than his actions and the response of the people; he wants God to *"try me, and know my thoughts"* (Psalm 139:23 KJV). In the beginning, David wanted to have a pure mind to go with his pure heart and a life that was pure before God. Technically, David was asking to be searched; he was saying for God to examine him to see if he has accurately represented his feelings and actions to the omniscient, omnipresent, and omnipotent God.

David ends the psalm, *"lead me in the way everlasting"* (Psalm 139:24 NKJV). That way he can have everlasting life in the presence of God. How blessed it must be for a man who comes to the end of his life knowing he can step from this life into the presence of God and enjoy eternity with the Lord Himself.

Chapter 10
Psalm 116: Rejoicing in God's Mercy

I love you Lord because You heard my prayer, and answered my request, and inclined Yourself to me. Therefore, I will pray to You always. The threat of death scared me, the prospect of hell was real; I went through agony and sorrow. Then I prayed for Your deliverance. You were gracious to me, and Your mercy saved me. You protected me in the hour of my need. I will rest in You Lord because You have saved my soul, taken away my fears, and kept my feet from falling. I will walk before You my Lord in integrity, I will testify of Your goodness, I repent because I believe in You. Now what can I give to You my Lord? I will drink Your cup of salvation. I will call on Your name, I will pay my vows before others. Lord, I will keep my promises to You, I will tell all the people of Your faithfulness.

—Psalm 116:1-14, author's paraphrase

Psalm 116 begins with the wonderful statement, *"I love the Lord,"* and shouldn't our love for the Lord always be a reaction for His great love to us? *"We love Him because He first loved us"* (1 John 4:19 NKJV).

However, here the psalmist is saying that he loves the Lord, *"because He has heard my voice and my supplications"* (Psalm 116:1). So our love to the Lord comes from His love to us. Remember, love begets love. And isn't that a wonderful motivation to pray or talk to Him?

Because God has heard us, the psalmist comes to the conclusion, *"I will call upon Him as long as I live"* (Psalm 116:2 NKJV). That's a great reason to pray in your time of need, to pray when you have no known need—to always pray (see 1 Thessalonians 5:17).

Next, the psalmist gives three conditions or reasons that motivated him to call upon the Lord. First, "the sorrows of death." We do not know if this was the death of fellow warrior or family member or the death of someone else. But death moved him to call upon God. Second, *"the pains of hell gat hold upon me"* (Psalm 116:3 KJV). What happened to the psalmist that he thought about the fierce torments of death or even the possibility of hell? Whatever it was, his love toward God motivated him to pray. And third, *"I found trouble and sorrow"* (Psalm 116:3 KJV). Even though he was alive, he faced troubles and difficulties, and now he could express his love to the Lord.

Prayer is never out of season but always is acceptable in your approach to God. So the psalmist confessed, *"then I called upon the name of the Lord"* (Psalm 116:4).

Very quickly the psalmist turns to the goodness of God and he exclaims, *"Gracious is the Lord, and righteous; yes, our God is merciful"* (Psalm 116:5 NKJV). Remember that grace is God giving us the exact opposite of what we deserve. We should always thank God for eternal life. We do not deserve it. Second, *righteous* means that God is always right and knows what is right, does right, and rewards us when we do right things. Third, God is merciful—He gives us the exact opposite of what we deserve; He gives us His love and care.

When the psalmist said, *"The Lord preserves the simple"* (Psalm 116:6 NKJV), the word *simple* here does not carry the modern-day meaning, but rather means *pure*, without hypocrisy, and without guile. So when you walk before the Lord in purity, He preserves you and helps you.

Next, the psalmist talks about his soul: *"return to your rest,"* meaning he's turning to God from the horrors that have crashed down on him. Why? Because the Lord has been bountiful in dealing with him. Notice the threefold deliverance of the Lord. First, He delivered his soul from death; second, his eyes from tears; and third, his feet from falling (see Psalm 116:8). This threefold blessing means that God has given a complete deliverance.

The psalmist promises, *"I will walk before the Lord in the land of the living"* (Psalm 116:9 NKJV). This suggests he is going to walk in a godly way before people living and watching him. Perhaps his walk is influenced by God, if not influenced by the promise of Heaven itself. This psalmist puts his belief into words: *"I believed, therefore I spoke"* (Psalm 116:10 NKJV).

Next the psalmist asked the question, "*What shall I render to the Lord for all His benefits toward me?*" (Psalm 116:12). Notice the wisdom of the psalmist—he sets aside his problems and does not complain about his difficulties and suffering. Rather, he puts his eyes on God to praise God and worship Him for what He has done for him.

He gives a threefold answer. First, "*I will take up the cup of salvation.*" This means he will rejoice in his salvation as much as one is glad to receive a cup of water when thirsty. Second, he says he will "*call upon the name of the Lord.*" Here he will have access to God, open to talk to Him continually. And third, "*I will pay my vows to the Lord*" (Psalm 116:12-14 NKJV). And then the psalmist falls back on his threefold expressions to show the deep sincerity of his promise.

Was the psalmist facing death? We do not know who wrote Psalm 116. Some of the reformation writers thought it was David. However, most scholars say it was Hezekiah who was going through a deep valley. He faced the threat of a Babylonian invasion and destruction of his nation. He called upon God and asked for deliverance and God answered.

When the author wrote, "*Precious in the sight of the Lord is the death of His saints*" (Psalm 116:15 NKJV), was this Hezekiah who was thinking about how many of God's people would be slaughtered if the Babylonians destroyed Jerusalem and took the nation captive? Whereas humans are destressed at the death of a parent or anyone else in their immediate family, God is not destressed when one of His children die; rather, it is precious to Him. Why is it precious? Because that person is relieved of all human responsibility, and they are ushered immediately into God's presence and He enjoys them.

So immediately, the author says, "*Truly I am Your servant*" (Psalm 116:16 NKJV). God is reminded that whether we live or die, we belong to Him and upon our death we immediately are ushered into His presence.

Then the psalmist gives another threefold promise. First: "*I will offer to You the sacrifice of thanksgiving.*" Second: "*And will call upon the name of the Lord.*" Third: "*I will pay my vows to the Lord now in the presence of all His people*" (Psalm 116:17-18 NKJV).

What you find here is the response of grateful heart who is more concerned about giving to God than receiving for himself. He is more concerned about paying the vows he promised to God than his own protection and continuation in this life.

So what is the ultimate destiny of one who puts God first? He knows he will be "*In the courts of the Lord's house, in the midst of you, O Jerusalem*" (Psalm 116:19 NKJV).

ABOUT ELMER TOWNS

Dr. Elmer Towns has published more than 100 books, several accepted as college textbooks. He is also a recipient of the Gold Medallion Award awarded by the Christian Booksellers Association. He is cofounder of Liberty University, holds visiting professorship rank at five seminaries, and has received six honorary doctoral degrees. He earned a BS from Northwestern College, a MA from Southern Methodist University, a ThM from Dallas Theological Seminary, a MRE from Garrett Theological Seminary, and a DMin from Fuller Theological Seminary.

YOUR Prophetic
C O M M U N I T Y

Sign up for a **FREE** subscription to the Destiny Image digital magazine and get awesome content delivered directly to your inbox!

destinyimage.com/signup

Sign up for Cutting-Edge Messages that Supernaturally Empower You

• Gain valuable insights and guidance based on biblical principles
• Deepen your faith and understanding of God's plan for your life
• Receive regular updates and prophetic messages
• Connect with a community of believers who share your values and beliefs

Experience Fresh Video Content that Reveals Your Prophetic Inheritance

• Receive prophetic messages and insights
• Connect with a powerful tool for spiritual growth and development
• Stay connected and inspired on your faith journey

Listen to Powerful Podcasts that Propel You into God's Presence Every Day

• Deepen your understanding of God's prophetic assignment
• Experience God's revival power throughout your day
• Learn how to grow spiritually in your walk with God